WIDE RAI
SCIENCE STORIES 4

Michael Holt and Alan Ward

Oliver & Boyd

Illustrated by Tony Morris and Martin Salisbury
Map on p. 37 by David Simon

The photographs on pp. 46 and 50 are reproduced by courtesy of the Science Museum, London; the filmstrips on pp. 53 and 54 were provided by Barry Adamson.

Oliver & Boyd
Robert Stevenson House
1–3 Baxter's Place
Leith Walk
Edinburgh EH1 3BB
A Division of Longman Group Ltd

ISBN 0 05 003293 3

First published 1983

© Michael Holt and Alan Ward 1983
All rights reserved. No part of this publication may be reproduced, stored in a retrieval system, or transmitted, in any form or by any means, electronic, mechanical, photocopying, recording or otherwise, without the prior permission of the copyright owners.

Printed in Hong Kong
by Sheck Wah Tong Printing Press Ltd

Preface

This series is an attempt to introduce junior school children to important ideas and experiences in science through the medium of stories. It is not in any way a science course, but we hope that it may be helpful in expanding the range and content of children's reading and introducing them to the world of science. The stories have all been chosen to relate to the kind of ideas the intended young reader finds comprehensible and interesting.

The four books of the series are written for children of reading ages 7 + to 11 +. Book One is broadly suitable for children of reading age 7 + to 8 +, Book Two for 8 + to 9 +, Book Three for 9 + to 10 + and Book Four for 10 + to 11 +.

Contents

The Surgeon with Clean Hands   4
The Fast-spinning Machine Man   12
Will Giant Airships ever Fly Again?   20
The Talking Horse Mystery   27
The Bald Eagle   30
The Inventors of Photography   42
Photography — without a Camera   51
Why People called Movies "the Flicks"   53
Captain Purefoy and the Large Blue   55
Be a "Butterfly Watcher"   59
The Genius who Tamed Niagara Falls   61
Test Your Nerves with an Electric Circuit   70
The Story of S   72
Walking Down Memory Lane   77
Isaac Newton   78
Rainbows on the Ceiling   87
Halley's Comet   89
The Story of RADAR   92
Hiroshima   101
Jane and the Apes   105
The Caged Scientist   116
Index   127

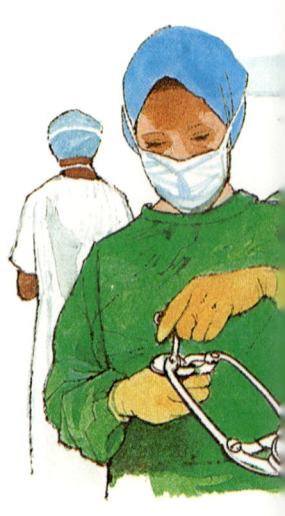

The Surgeon with Clean Hands

Think of an operation being carried out in a hospital today. The patient is covered in well-disinfected sheets. The surgeon has well-scrubbed hands and wears a smock, rubber gloves and a face-mask; so do all the nurses in the operating theatre. The nurses disinfect the scalpels the surgeon has to use. The walls of the theatre are disinfected. Even the air in the theatre is cleaned and filtered. This is all done in a modern hospital to reduce harmful germs that could kill the patient. But it was not always like that.

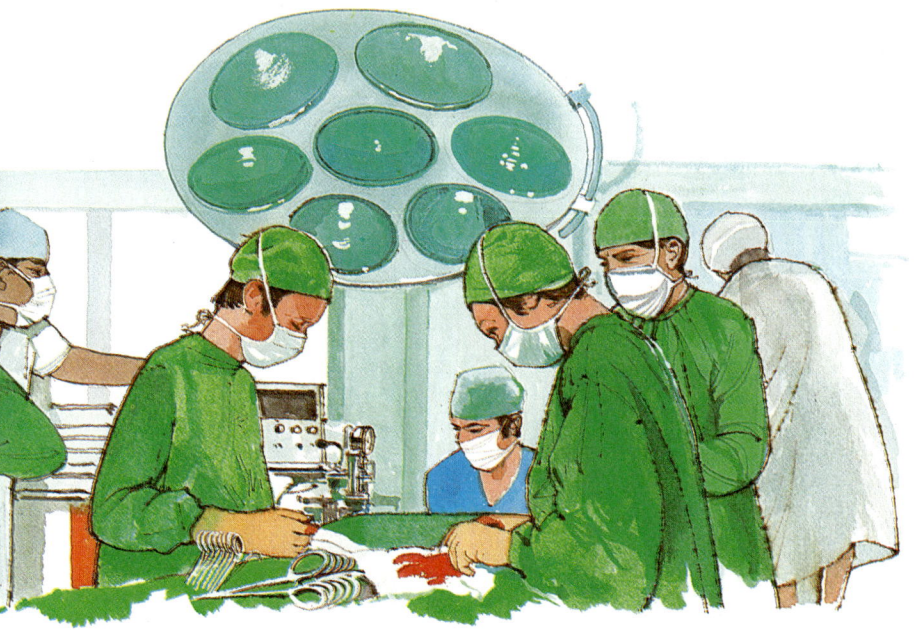

A hundred and fifty years ago hospitals were not so clean. Nor were the operating theatres. The surgeons, doctors and nurses certainly did not worry about cleanliness. They carried out operations in their street clothes. They might wear a butcher's apron but certainly not masks. They rarely washed their hands before an operation and they only rinsed the scalpels in water after an operation; they certainly did not disinfect them. So they carried infections from one patient to another. As for the rooms they operated in, they were more like theatres; set in a horse-shoe round the operating table was a steep bank of seats where other doctors in their ordinary clothes sat and watched the operations.

Small wonder then that patients died like flies after hospital operations simply because hospitals

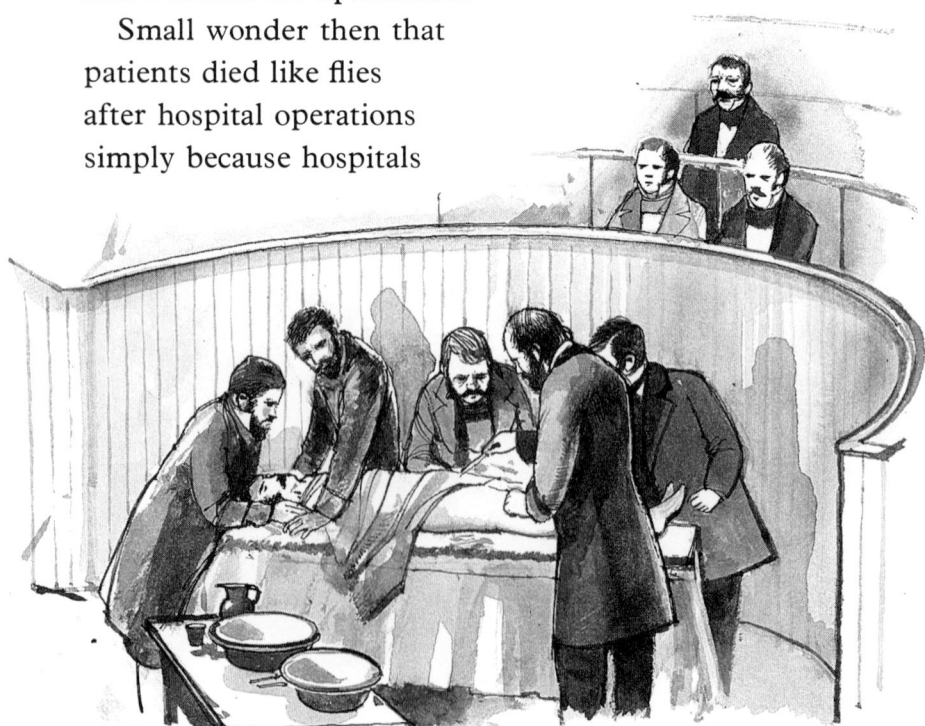

were so unclean and so unhygienic. Most surgeons had given up hope of doing anything about it. But not Joseph Lister! He was the first surgeon to have clean hands and he led the fight for clean hospitals.

• • • • • •

Joseph Lister was born in 1827, one of seven children, into a lively Quaker family. His parents taught him to fight for what he thought was right. His father was a scientist who improved the microscope and he passed on to Joseph his interest in animals and plants. There were always pets about the house for Joseph to study. There were ordinary ones such as dogs, cats and rabbits. There were farm animals: chicks, a cow and calves. Then there were more unusual pets: carrier pigeons, rats, deer and silkworms. Joseph and his brothers and sisters all cared for their pets. Joseph learnt to use his father's microscope and by the age of fourteen he was skilled at dissecting and studying small animals. This gave him the idea of becoming a surgeon.

At that time surgeons did not receive special training. A doctor who was interested in surgery learnt by working with other surgeons and watching them operate. This was how Lister learnt surgery and in 1852 he passed the exam that made him a fully-qualified surgeon. He first worked in London, then in Edinburgh with his older friend, the surgeon James Syme.

He soon realised why most patients died after an operation. It was not the surgeon's knife that killed them, but the infection in the wounds that nearly always followed. Other surgeons may have noticed this. But if they did, they left it at that. They did not seek a reason for it. Lister not only noticed it, he thought of a reason. He thought that wounds became infected from bits of dirt and chemicals that got into them. Encouraged by his friend Syme, Lister decided to do research into inflammation in wounds. It was this research that led to Lister making one of the greatest discoveries in surgery.

The real cause of inflammation in wounds was simply germs. Lister did not realise that these germs were in the hospital air, on the scalpels and knives or the bandages. Nonetheless he realised that it was vitally important to keep wounds clean. He made sure patients had clean sheets; he opened windows to let in fresh air. He made doctors and nurses wash their hands in soap and water before carrying out an operation. He tried to get surgeons to do the same, but some of them were enraged at the idea. As professional surgeons, they thought they were clean enough already!

Lister worked hard to make his hospital a cleaner place. As a result deaths from infected wounds dropped. But, unlike other surgeons, Lister did not rest satisfied. He was sure there was a cause for infected wounds. He was determined to find it.

In 1865 he found the clue he was looking for. He was reading through some of the writings of Louis

Louis Pasteur   Joseph Lister

Pasteur, the great French scientist. Pasteur had shown that germs brought infection. Lister wondered how to keep germs out of wounds. If he could do that, the wounds would not become infected, inflamed, and kill the patient. He had heard that carbolic acid was being used to disinfect the drains and sewers of Carlisle. So he decided to try carbolic acid on wounds and see if it stopped them becoming inflamed.

In those days carbolic acid was a thick, horrible-looking fluid, dark brown in colour and smelling strongly of tar. It was hard to believe that it would keep open wounds clean. All the same Lister tried it out. On the twelfth of August 1865 he used carbolic acid as an antiseptic when he operated on a man with a broken leg. He had the air sprayed with carbolic, all the instruments washed in it and the bandages soaked in it. The man's broken bone and the wound

both healed fast and well. There was no sign of infection. Other operations using carbolic brought the same results. In the next two years he did not lose a single patient from infection after surgery. Lister had beaten the germs.

Despite his success, some of his fellow-doctors were not impressed. They did not believe in his new antiseptic treatment for wounds. Some called his work useless. Others used carbolic acid on old bandages; they did not change the bandages each time the wound was checked. One surgeon even said that "germs" did not exist and refused to try carbolic acid at all.

Lister was saddened by these attacks but not disheartened. He carried on with his work, first in Edinburgh and then in London. Always he made the hospitals where he worked safer places. Always he tried to persuade other doctors of the value of clean-

liness. Slowly his ideas were accepted. By 1879 he had won his great victory. Other doctors and surgeons throughout Britain accepted that Lister was right and great efforts were made to improve standards of cleanliness in hospitals.

Lister himself was loaded with honours. He became surgeon to Queen Victoria and President of great scientific societies. In 1897 he was made a baron — Baron Lister of Lyme Regis. He was the first doctor to be honoured in this way but it did not change him. He continued to work for safer medicine and safer hospitals. When he died in 1912 hospitals were clean and airy places, quite unlike the dangerous and filthy buildings of seventy years before. This change was Lister's doing, but he himself always said that he owed his ideas to the great Pasteur. For Joseph Lister was not only a great scientist — he was also a humble man.

The Fast-spinning Machine Man

Until two hundred years ago, all cotton cloth was spun and woven by hand in the home. Spinning and weaving like this was known as a Cottage Industry. Then came the Industrial Revolution and with it new machines and new methods. The new machines made spinning and weaving quicker, cheaper and more profitable. Crowds of workers tended these machines, no longer in their homes, but in big cheerless factories.

One of the first to organise such a factory was Richard Arkwright. He set up the first cotton mill in the world at Cromford in Derbyshire. It was powered by a water-wheel and employed three hundred workers.

Cotton has always been important. Look around you and see how many fabrics are made of it. Think of all the other cotton goods — from tiny first-aid bandages to vast hotel carpets. Of all the countless fabrics, natural and artificial (such as nylon), cotton is by far the most popular. Today three-quarters of the people in the world wear cotton clothes!

Cotton is grown in more than sixty countries in the world. It has been spun and woven for at least five thousand years — the earliest known piece of cotton cloth is dated 3000 B.C., from the Indus Valley civilisation.

Spinning itself is one of the oldest crafts in the

world. For thousands of years people used distaffs and spindles for spinning cotton. The distaff was a smooth stick with a notch at the top for holding one end of the cotton thread. The early Egyptians used spindles for making fine cotton. Today Egyptian cotton is sold widely.

Distaff

Spindle

Spinning was done on a spindle until the middle of the sixteenth century, when the spinning wheel was invented. The spinner (or *spinster*) worked a foot pedal to turn the wheel, which pulled the cotton in a fine thread from a spindle holding the cotton to be spun. The spinner pulled the cotton out by hand, and the faster she pedalled, the finer the yarn she spun.

When the yarn had been spun, it was woven into cloth on a simple wooden hand-loom. Weaving was faster than spinning, even after the spinning wheel had been invented, and this had always created a "bottleneck" in the making of cloth. Then the flying shuttle was invented by John Kay in 1733; weaving could be done even faster, and the spinner really lagged behind.

At last, about 1764, a spinning machine was invented by James Hargreaves, a Lancashire weaver, and spinning took a great leap forward. The machine was called a "spinning jenny" (from *gin*, the Lancashire word for engine) and it could spin sixteen or more threads at a time, instead of the single thread that a spinning wheel could produce. But it had one big drawback — it could only spin coarse thread. It could not produce the fine yarn needed for dresses and shirts.

And this was where Richard Arkwright came in. For he managed to turn the spinning jenny into a machine that would produce very fine and strong cotton threads.

He was born in Preston, Lancashire, in 1732, the son of poor parents and one of a family of thirteen children. He started work early, and perhaps his background played some part in his powerful urge to get on in the world — to live in a mansion and ride in a carriage; to be a member of the "gentry" of those days. Although he was a rough sort of man and quite uneducated (at fifty he was still learning to spell), he achieved his aim long before he died.

He started as apprentice to a barber and wigmaker in Bolton, Lancashire, but even as a young man he had great initiative. He hit upon a way of dyeing hair different colours for making wigs, and he became a dealer in hair for wigs, travelling from town to town in search of such hair.

Then one day he overheard a conversation that was

to change his life ... and change the whole spinning industry. He overheard someone saying, "You know, there's a small fortune to be made out of spinning cotton. All that's needed is a machine to spin cotton faster. The person who can invent a really fast spinning machine will make a lot of money."

There and then Richard Arkwright made up his mind that *he* was going to be that person. He was going to invent a spinning machine and make his fortune.

Although Arkwright was a good mechanic, his strength lay in developing other people's ideas — and in organisation.

First, he set about finding out how the most up-to-date spinning machine worked. This was James Hargreaves' spinning jenny. He went to look at one in action, and quickly saw several ways to speed it up. The spinning jenny was hand-operated. Its success lay in the high-speed drive for the spindle and in the number of spindles used. Arkwright decided

that it needed more power to turn the spindles. His first thought was horse power, but to change the pull of a horse into the movement of wheels going round, he would need some form of clockwork.

As luck would have it, he became friendly with a clockmaker, John Kay, who taught him how to make clockwork cogs and wheels that turned one another.

At this time, Arkwright was working as much as sixteen hours a day, for his heart was set on achieving his ambitions. By the end of 1767 he had made a small model of his new machine, and it worked very well — for a model.

He showed the model to a businessman, John Smalley, who was so impressed that he agreed to lend Richard Arkwright the money to make a full-sized version. This he did in a few months, but by that time there was trouble among the cotton workers in Lancashire. The workers were afraid that they would lose their jobs, because new machines such as Hargreaves' spinning jenny would need fewer people to look after them. So they rioted and started breaking up the machines.

Because of this, Arkwright decided to leave Lancashire. He moved to Nottingham, where he found two wealthy hosiers (makers of stockings) to back him — Samuel Need and Jedediah Strutt. Together the three men set up a factory to use Arkwright's new roller spinning machine. The new machine could make thread as fine and tough as they wanted, and much faster than ever before.

Now Arkwright needed power to drive his machines, and he used horses to turn a horse-capstan — an upright beam of wood to which a pair of horses were harnessed. The beam turned as the horses walked round in a circle, and it was linked to the spinning machines by a series of cogs and wheels — an enormous piece of clockwork. The horse-powered factory was very successful, and it turned out cotton yarn that sold well in Nottinghamshire.

There was a snag to using horses to drive the machines, however. Not only did they need stabling and feeding, they also got tired, and several pairs of horses were needed in a day to keep the spinning machines going. Arkwright thought about using wind power, but this was not reliable enough. So he decided to use water-power.

At Cromford, in Derbyshire, he built a cotton spinning mill with a big water-wheel which was driven by the river. This was the very first water-powered cotton mill in the world, and Arkwright's machines started to be called "water-frames".

So successful was the water-frame machine that Richard Arkwright went on to build other factories in Derbyshire, in Lancashire, and in New Lanark, in Scotland. He built ten in the Midlands alone, and he was now well on his way to making his fortune.

By this time he was so busy that he used to travel with four horses at great speed. He began work at five o'clock in the morning and went on till nine o'clock at night. And as if that were not enough, he also studied hard — learning to write and to improve his grammar. Because he worked so hard and such long hours himself, he thought nothing of asking his workers to work a fourteen-hour day!

In 1781, Arkwright's patent on his water-frame was challenged. In 1769 he had taken out a patent on his invention to show that he was the first man to have thought of it, and he was charging royalties. But when his patent was challenged, it was proved that the water-frame was not his own invention — other people had invented the various parts of the machine he had put together.

As a result, Arkwright's patent was cancelled; but his factories continued to prosper — and their owner, rough-mannered and shrewd, prospered with them.

His water-frame began to be used more widely, so that England became the richest cotton-spinning country in the world. Because he had helped to make England rich, he was knighted in 1786, and became Sir Richard Arkwright. Arkwright was not a likeable man. He was greedy and pot-bellied and interested only in his own profits. He cared little for others, but when he died in 1792 he was a wealthy and honoured man. Ruthless ambition and sly cunning had taken him far from his own humble beginnings.

Will Giant Airships ever Fly Again?

When we think of air raids, we think of heavy bomber aircraft, escorted by fast fighter planes. But the first air raids were made by Zeppelin airships sent by the Germans to bomb British cities in the First World War. They did little damage, however, because many of them were shot down in flames by British aircraft. Special incendiary bullets were used to set fire to the highly dangerous hydrogen gas which held the airships in the air.

Some of the "super-Zeppelins" were over two hundred metres long, but most of the space inside them was taken up by large, balloon-like gasbags. Each Zeppelin was commanded by a captain, who rode in a cabin mounted underneath the airship's fish-shaped hull.

As weapons the Zeppelins failed, but as lighter-than-air flying machines they had already proved very successful long before the First World War. Up to 1914, ten thousand passengers had flown safely in airships designed and built by the rich Count Ferdinand von Zeppelin. Other countries also built airships, but the German Zeppelins were the most advanced in design.

The two most famous German airships were the *Graf Zeppelin* and the *Hindenburg*. These airships carried passengers across the Atlantic Ocean in the days before aeroplanes were powerful enough to do the crossing in one hop. In 1929, the *Graf Zeppelin* flew right round the world in 21 days, 5 hours and 31 minutes.

On the fourth of May 1937, the *Hindenburg* left Frankfurt in what was then Nazi Germany, on a routine flight to America. There were ninety-seven people on board, of which only thirty-six were passengers, each person paying £86 for a single fare. (In those days, that was nearly as much as most people earned in a year.)

Before take-off, the *Hindenburg* was held steady by hundreds of men pulling on ropes. After the captain gave the order to let go, a shower of water was dropped from the airship, to make it weigh less. Then it was driven away by humming propellers fixed to its gigantic hull.

As fuel was used up by the engines, the airship picked up more water from the clouds, to balance the

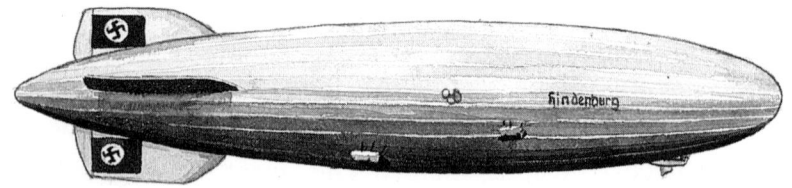

The *Hindenburg*

weight lost. The height above ground was checked by pinging down sound pulses which were reflected back as echoes from the earth. By knowing the speed of sound, it was possible to measure altitude by timing how long the sound took to be echoed back again to the airship. The swastika-painted ship swept the ground ahead with a bright searchlight as it droned over Europe's cities by night.

Travelling on the *Hindenburg* was like being in a spacious flying hotel. Those on board could look down through wide picture windows to watch the world passing below.

The passengers slept in two-berth cabins, fitted with writing tables and basins with hot and cold running water. A chef cooked excellent meals, which were served in the grand dining saloon. The tables there

were decorated with fresh flowers, and there was even dancing to music from an aluminium piano. There was a library on board, and a church service was held on Sundays. All this went on high up in the clouds above a raging sea — nearly fifty years ago!

On its arrival in America, the *Hindenburg* flew over the Statue of Liberty, the harbour of New York and the skyscrapers of Manhattan Island. Then it ran southward, losing height slowly as some of the gas was released from its gasbags. The great airship headed for Lakehurst, New Jersey.

• • • • • •

Radio broadcaster Herb Morrison watched spellbound as the mammoth German airship loomed over the landing field at Lakehurst. Herb could hardly hide the sense of wonder and excitement in his voice as he described the preparations for landing: "The ship is riding majestically towards us like some great feather, riding as though it was mighty proud of its place in aviation ..."

Herb's "feather" had just flown across the Atlantic in three days. It was 242 metres long — a silver torpedo as long as a street of houses flying in the evening sky.

But then the tone of Herb's voice abruptly changed, to send a thrill of horror through his listeners ... "It's burst into flames ... It's crashing ... Oh ... Get out of the way please ... This is one of the worst catastrophes in the world."

    The proud symbol of Hitler's Germany was a glowing cloud of yellow fire and melting metal. Sparks of static electricity shooting between the airship and its tall mooring mast had set fire to hydrogen gas leaking from one of its gasbags, and caused a huge explosion.

    Herb's listeners could tell that he was in tears before the broadcast finished. And so ended the first chapter in the story of airships.

• • • • • • •

Sixty-two people managed to escape alive from the burning airship as it settled — not too suddenly — on the ground, because much of the intense heat was carried upwards with the flames. Engineers said that after the *Hindenburg* disaster and other bad airship crashes, airships would never fly again. They were unsafe. They broke up too easily in storms, and were too much of a fire risk — unless they were lifted by non-explosive helium gas, which was much too expensive to use. The discussions and arguments went on until the Second World War began soon afterwards.

Aeroplanes proved much more reliable as weapons of destruction, and airships were almost forgotten, although the Americans sometimes used small airships for sea patrol work.

Now, however, some engineers are beginning to think that, with the use of modern technology and helium gas (which is cheaper and more plentiful than it used to be), airships could be very useful in the world of the future. They are already being used once more for certain specialised purposes such as television photography.

It is true that airships are much slower than aeroplanes, but they would be cheaper to run, and there are many instances where they could be much more useful. An airship fitted out like a hospital for example could be flown to the site of an earthquake in some remote place in the world within a day or two.

Freight carrying by lorry and train is expensive and inconvenient, especially where the cargo has to be sent to places where there are few roads and railways. Lorries and trains also use up a lot of fuel and cause air pollution and nerve-shattering noise. Even ships can only go where there is water, but silently-running airships can travel in the ocean of air that connects every place on earth. By airship, tonnes of tinned food could be carried from London to Milan in Italy in just seven hours — directly to where the food was needed.

Airships of the future would not depend on landing fields. Those airships could be built with super-strong new metals and coverings; they could be computer-controlled, and kept aloft by fireproof helium gas. They could be driven by quiet diesel or nuclear engines, lifting payloads of up to a thousand tonnes. They could stay in the air for years, without landing . . . They would be able to hover above the ground while they were loaded and unloaded by special shuttle helicopters . . . .

There is a strong chance that chapter two in the story of airships is about to begin!

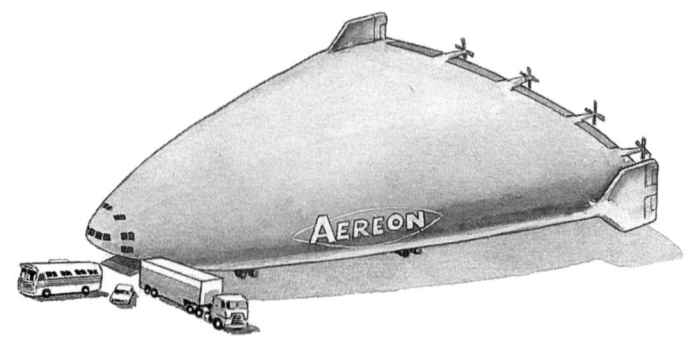

The Talking Horse Mystery

Clever Hans was a horse — and he could answer questions! He did not actually talk, but counted or spelt out answers by stamping a hoof. For example, if you asked the horse, "What is four times two?" Clever Hans would know that the answer was eight, and would stamp a hoof eight times — at least, that is what people thought was happening.

Although there have been reports from time to time throughout history about a "talking horse", Clever Hans is one of the most famous. He lived early this century, and he belonged to Wilhelm Von Osten, an elderly gentleman living in Berlin. Many learned professors believed that the amazing horse could do sums and answer questions about world events, but there was one man who was not convinced.

He was Oskar Pfungst, a scientist who was interested in the mental powers of animals. Since Wilhelm Von Osten believed completely in Clever Hans, he was willing to let the horse be tested by Herr Pfungst.

To start with, the scientist noticed that Clever Hans never gave an answer that Wilhelm Von Osten did not know himself. Oskar Pfungst wondered, could Wilhelm be cheating by giving secret signals to his wonderful horse?

The scientist went on with his tests, and this time he covered Clever Hans's eyes. When Wilhelm asked his blindfolded horse to solve a multiplication sum, and to spell the name of the late Queen of England, the "talking hoof" was still. Now why? Was Clever Hans upset by the eye-shield? Then Herr Pfungst thought, perhaps the horse needed to *see* Wilhelm! He had noticed, however, that Wilhelm did not touch the horse, or make the slightest sound to give Clever Hans any clues. If it *was* a trick, how was it done?

Then Oskar Pfungst made yet another important observation. Clever Hans only started stamping when Wilhelm bent forward, ever so slightly. The sharp-eyed horse noticed this tiny movement that humans were not observant enough to see. He stopped stamping when he saw that Wilhelm had relaxed. No one had ever noticed this before, because their astonished eyes had always been focused on Clever Hans rather than his master. The scientist had guessed that Wilhelm was signalling — but that he did it unconsciously, that is, without knowing that he was doing it.

To test his guess, Pfungst pretended to be a horse, and asked his friends to think of a question that could be answered by a certain number of hand taps. When they had thought of a question, his friends became a little tense and bent forward slightly. This unconscious action was a kind of "body language" that Herr Pfungst had learnt to understand.

He began tapping slowly, until his questioners relaxed. This told him that he had tapped enough times to signal the number of taps they had been thinking of for the answer. Then he stopped tapping.

His friends were completely baffled. They thought

Oskar was reading their minds when really, like a good scientist, he was only being very observant.

In 1904, Herr Pfungst published his explanation of the "talking horse" mystery. One man, in his turn, refused to believe *him* — Wilhelm Von Osten!

The Bald Eagle

Have you ever seen a proud, fierce eagle on American coins or flags? It is the bald eagle, the American national bird. It is called the bald eagle — not because it is truly bald, but because its white-feathered head makes it look bald from a distance.

One man, Daniel Mannix, spent years of his life watching these eagles all over America. He watched them as chicks and as adults. He saw them learn to fly and learn to hunt. He watched them at different nests all over America. He talked to other people who knew and loved eagles. Then, from all he had learnt he made up this story of one young eagle.

• • • • • •

High in an elm tree overlooking Chesapeake Bay on the Atlantic coast of North America was a great nest of sticks and branches. The nest was three metres across and it was the home of a pair of bald eagles.

Early every year they came back to it to lay their eggs and bring up a new family. This year there were three eggs and in the spring three eaglets hatched out. One was the "hero" of our story, the second his sister, the largest and strongest of the three, and the third their weakling brother.

From the moment they were hatched they needed feeding. The mother eagle and her mate were busy all day hunting for small animals to feed the baby birds. Every day the young eagles ate their own weight in food and every day they fought each other for the largest pieces. Because they were strong the young eagle and his sister could usually eat their fill. Not so their weaker brother. He had to go hungry.

When the eaglets were a month old their flying feathers began to push through the soft down on their bodies. This made them hungrier than ever. If they went without food for even a few hours their feathers would be weakened. The fights in the great nest became even fiercer. Mostly the sister won and she took most of the food brought to the nest. The young eagle took much of the rest and he found ways of robbing his sister. When she stood over a dead fish and tore at it with her beak he ate the part of the fish sticking out behind her. His cunning kept him strong and healthy, but their weakling brother had neither strength nor cunning. Each day he grew weaker.

One day there was very little food to eat. The parent birds had gone out hunting early in the morning but they had not returned and there was no food in the nest. All three birds were starving. Suddenly the young eagle was attacked by his sister. Fearful, he backed away to the edge of the nest. His sister turned instead on the weakling brother, killing him with one blow of her beak. Hungrily, she tore at his body. After that the young eagle watched his sister very, very carefully. He did not want to share his brother's fate. He determined to leave the nest as soon as possible and began to practise flying. First he made jumps across the nest. When he spread his wings, the air blowing over them lifted him into the air and he could float above the nest. His sister was heavier and less skilful and she learnt more slowly.

Perhaps the parent birds had seen these jumps. Perhaps they just knew that it was time the young eagles began to fly. One day when they returned with food they did not drop it into the nest and fly away to catch more. Instead the mother eagle flew round and round the nest, holding a pigeon in her claws. The young eagles leaned out of the nest, pecking greedily at the pigeon. Then the young male eagle leaned too far. He missed the pigeon and fell out of the nest. He screamed with fear and his wings flapped wildly. His mother and father could not hold him up but they flew close enough to touch him with their wings. Somehow their shrill cries helped him. Instead of flapping his wings wildly the young eagle spread them wide. At once his fall stopped and he began to soar on the air. His newly-grown flying feathers were

strong enough to take his weight even though he could not control his flight. He glided down towards the earth and crashed heavily into a tree. There he sat uneasily on a branch while his parents fed him small pieces of food. That afternoon his sister also left the nest for the first time. She was less lucky or less skilful than her brother and her flight ended on the ground. There she had to stay, for she had not learnt how to take off from the ground or fly upwards.

Night fell. The young male slept uneasily on his perch. He was used to the broad, safe platform of the nest and the company of the other birds. His sister slept on the ground below, some way off. It was a quiet night and the only sound that disturbed the young bird was the baying of a pack of dogs on the trail of a deer. But next morning there was no sign of his sister. The dogs had found her and there were only a few feathers on the ground.

During the next week the young eagle learnt to use his wings. He learnt how to glide and soar, how to turn and dip and swoop. He learnt how to fly upwards, and found his way back to the nest. He began to find food for himself. Eagles will eat almost any meat or fish, alive or dead, and at first he looked for easy catches. One morning he saw below him some vultures eating a dead dog. He flew down, drove away the vultures and started to tear at the raw meat. What he did not know was that he was on a road. Probably the dog had been knocked down by a car. So he made no move when another car came towards him. It could have run him over, but instead it stopped with a great squeal of brakes and a man jumped out. Still the eagle took no notice. He had not learnt to be afraid of humans. Then the man picked up a stone and threw it at him, hitting his right wing. Painfully he took off and slowly made his way back to the nest. He had learnt two things: roads and men were not to be trusted.

When he was able to fly properly again the young eagle began to hunt with his parents. He watched how his father swooped down on prey and how he killed it. The young bird's first kill of his own was a banded water snake. He saw the snake in a glade and flew down in a long, low glide. He picked it up in his talons

and carried it back towards the nest. The snake twisted round in his grip and tried to bite him, but could not pierce his scaly leg armour.

The young eagle flew on and up to the nest. There he stayed, still grasping the snake. He didn't know what to do with it and had to wait for his father to show him how to kill it. The older bird bit the snake's head off and together they ate the snake. From then on the eagle always killed snakes instantly, biting their heads off with his beak as he had seen his father do.

That autumn he learnt to catch muskrats swimming in the swamps. He learnt to glide in silently and swiftly from behind the muskrat so that the animal could not see him or hear him. For the eagle, catching muskrats was more dangerous than catching snakes. The muskrat could bite through even the eagle's leg armour and the young bird had to grab the animal in one claw only.

His most difficult lesson was learning how to fish.

His parents sat for hours on trees by the water's edge, watching the surface of the water. Then, suddenly, one of them would fly down to the water, dive into it and come out with a struggling fish in its talons. The young eagle tried to copy them. Catching fish seemed easy, but it wasn't and he missed every time. He was annoyed and puzzled. It looked so easy. He had to learn to allow for the bending of light when it enters water. This made the fish seem to be a few centimetres away from where it actually was. So the eagle would fly down and grab for two "fish", one with each foot. And so he learnt to catch his fish every time.

From his parents he learnt other ways of hunting. He learnt how to outwit ospreys and steal their food. He watched for pheasants and ducks wounded by hunters' guns and picked them up from the ground or water.

Then winter came and with it harsh winds and heavy snow. It became harder and harder to find food. Few small animals came out into the snow and the sea was so rough and stormy that fishing became impossible. The eagles grew more and more hungry. One day when they had had no food for days, the father eagle decided to fly south to warmer lands. He flew inland, followed by the other two birds. For hour after hour they flew. They spent that night in a maple tree and next morning they found a dead deer. They ate their fill of the meat and it saved their lives. Without that food they would have died.

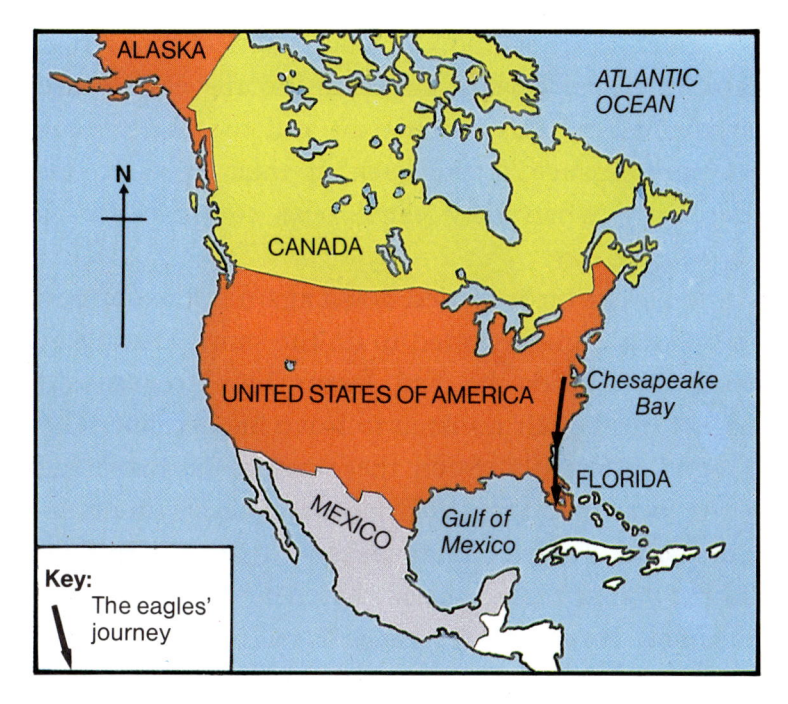

They flew south again the next day, following a current of warm air. This led them down to Florida and there they spent the winter. The warm, wet marshes on the Florida coast are full of fish, snakes and flocks of slow-flying birds and the eagles fed well all winter.

In February the eagles began to be restless. They made short flights around the trees, almost as if they were waiting for some sign. Then one day, a steady wind was blowing northwards and the parent birds set off, followed by their son. They were heading back to their nest on the Atlantic coast, 1500 kilometres away.

How could they possibly know where to go? The answer lies in the magnetism of the earth. The earth is a giant magnet and its magnetism changes from place to place. Special tubes inside the eagle's eyes are affected by this magnetism and the eagles could feel the pressure at the back of their eyes. It only went away when they came near to their nest in Chesapeake Bay.

The parent birds settled down again in the old nest. The young eagle expected to do the same. During the winter in Florida he had learnt how to hunt for himself but he felt no need to leave his parents. They thought differently. Soon there would be more eggs in the nest and they did not want their young son to be around then. They began to drive him away and the young eagle realised that if he stayed he might be killed. He left the nest and set off on his own. During the next few years the eagle lived and hunted in different areas of North America. He became a skilled hunter.

One day, flying above the Mississippi, he spotted a lone female eagle. She was perched on a large nest on top of an old hickory tree. There was no other eagle in sight and for a time the two birds watched each other. Then the female flew over to the oak tree where the male was perched. She settled on the branch next to him. She was bigger than he was, and they sat there for several minutes, staring at each other.

Then the female took off from the oak tree, giving short, harsh cries and spreading her beautiful wings in the sunlight. The male followed and they flew together, circling and soaring and swooping in the clear air. Suddenly the female stopped the game and flew off, calling the male to follow her. She led him on, flying almost too fast for him. She flew to the big nest on top of the hickory tree and the male landed beside her. The two eagles sat almost touching, resting after the flight. This nest was to be their home for the rest of their lives.

The eagles' courtship lasted all summer. Every day they dived and spun in mock battle, learning to respect each other's skill in the air. In the autumn the flying displays stopped. The two birds turned to remaking the big nest. They fetched branches, twigs, and soft grass and wove them into a strong, flat nest. In the centre was a hollow lined with soft hay and feathers. The nest was ready for the eggs the female would soon lay.

The first of the chalky-white eggs was laid on a morning in the summer, followed by a second three days later. For the next fortnight the female eagle did not leave the nest. She sat on the eggs to keep them warm and her mate hunted for food and fed her. After two weeks she was able to leave the nest and the male sat on the eggs to keep them warm. For a month more they took it in turns to sit on the eggs. Then the tiny eagle chicks hatched out. They were no bigger than a robin in size but much more hungry. Every day the parents went hunting and every day the young eagles ate their fill.

So began the long careful business of bringing up their own baby eagles. Soon the eaglets would learn to fly and hunt for themselves. They too would leave the nest in search of mates of their own. For year after year this pattern would be repeated. More eggs would be laid, more chicks would be born.

• • • • • •

Great eagles like these live for many years in the wild. A bullet from a hunter's gun or an egg collector's greedy hands are almost the only things adult birds need fear. Nonetheless the number of bald eagles in America has been going down. Some are killed by hunters every year, some die of old age, others die in accidents. These deaths would not matter so much if there were plenty of young birds to take their place. But there are not. Many eggs never hatch out. The baby birds are dead before they are born, killed by the chemical poisons in their parents' food. There are fewer places where the eagles can hunt in safety. The great forests and wild places where the eagles live are fewer today than they were even twenty years ago.

Americans do not want to see their national bird follow the dodo into extinction. They have set up nature reserves where the birds can live in safety. There are even some controls on the use of the chemicals that poison the birds' food. There is hope once more for that proud bird, the bald eagle.

The Inventors of Photography

Today, the photographer is an artist. He creates and balances a picture, using his camera as a tool to achieve his aim. He rarely thinks of the time, thought and patient experiment which brought photography to its present perfection.

Most great inventions are really the work of many people. The work of one builds on the efforts of another. Often several people, in different parts of the world, are working on the same idea at the same time, each thinking it is his idea alone. All this is especially true of the invention of photography.

Photography means "writing with light", and it would be hard to imagine modern life without it. Light is a form of energy which can produce changes in the appearance of certain chemicals. Materials such as curtains and book covers lose their colours when they are exposed to bright sunlight for a long time.

Prove this for yourself. Put a number of things — say, a comb, a shell, and a coin — on a sheet of coloured sugar paper, and leave them in the sun for a few days. When you lift the things off, their shapes will have been "photographed" on the paper. Exposed parts of the paper fade, but the parts covered by the objects remain unchanged. Of course this would be a poor way to make pictures, but it does show how light energy can cause changes that can leave records of real shapes.

The story of photography began more than a hundred and fifty years ago, when a Frenchman called Joseph Niepce made the first camera. He described it as "an artificial eye that is quite simply a little square box fifteen centimetres on each side, fitted with an extension tube that carries a lens." He pointed his box camera out of the window of his workshop and allowed the lens to focus light on to a "film" inside the camera. The film was a piece of paper coated with a chemical called silver chloride.

In this way Niepce created a crude photograph. It showed the window frame, and a bird house in his garden. Unfortunately, the light parts of the picture came out black, and the dark bits stayed white. He had made what today we call a negative — but he couldn't "fix" the photograph. When it was exposed to the light again, the whole negative turned black, and his photograph was lost.

Niepce did not worry too much about this problem. He wanted to make a more natural-looking picture, with the light bits light and the dark bits dark. He started to look for a dark chemical that would turn light when light rays hit it. He succeeded by using a plate made of pewter metal, coated with a black chemical called bitumen of Judea. The exposure time for the actual photography was very long indeed — about eight hours! Normally the bitumen dissolved in lavender oil, but light rays changed it into a form that would not dissolve. So when the photograph had been taken, the picture could be fixed by simply dissolving the bitumen which hadn't been changed by light. From this exposed and washed plate, Niepce was able to make a black and white normal-looking positive image. He took the world's first photograph in 1826.

The method, however, took far too long and was clumsy. During the eight hours that the picture was being taken, the sun's position altered so much that sunlight appeared on opposite walls on buildings in the picture! Today's cameras, using different methods, are fantastically faster. They can take pictures in thousandths of a second. It would almost be true to say that, with modern photography, we can make time stand still.

Niepce's experiments attracted the attention of a showman, another Frenchman named Louis Daguerre. He earned his living by putting on entertainments called Dioramas — very complicated and dramatic three-dimensional natural scenes, with special lighting.

Joseph Niepce   Louis Daguerre

Daguerre was a businessman who knew that a fortune awaited the inventor of a quick and easy way to take photographs. He himself had done some experiments like Niepce's early ones with silver chloride. Daguerre saw that Niepce was well on the way to inventing practical photography, so very cleverly he persuaded him to become his business partner. In this way he managed to learn all about Niepce's work, without providing any new ideas of his own.

Niepce and Daguerre began to use copper plates coated with silver iodide as "films" inside their cameras, but the photographic images turned out to be negatives. For the Frenchmen this was no good, because they were only interested in producing positives. Nevertheless, when Niepce died in 1833, Daguerre knew some of the essential ideas that would help him to become the world's first practical photographer.

Then he had a stroke of luck. One day he left a number of under-exposed silver iodide plates in a cupboard containing some spilt mercury. When he opened the cupboard next day, he saw that the negatives on the plates had turned into positive realistic pictures! The mercury had evaporated and reacted with chemicals on the plates, to reverse the images.

Now Daguerre had only one problem left. He had to find a way to fix the pictures so that they would not be spoilt by sunlight. He knew very little chemistry, but luck was with him once more. By trying different solutions, he found out that a solution of common salt fixed pictures on the plates. Although the new invention was largely based on Niepce's work, Daguerre named the process after himself.

Daguerreotypes were praised by people all over the world. The delicate black and white pictures, fixed on the metal plates,

A Daguerreotype.
A portrait
of Madame Daguerre.

measured about eighteen centimetres by twelve. The detail was so clear that a Daguerreotype could be magnified fifty times to show the finer points. Anyone was allowed to make the pictures, and for his part in the invention, Daguerre was awarded a pension of £6000 a year by the French government.

• • • • • •

While Daguerre was busy in France, other scientists were working on photography in England. The most important of these was a brilliantly clever and rich man named William Fox Talbot, who owned Lacock Abbey, a beautiful house near Bath. His interests covered both arts and sciences. He wrote articles about the science of light and colour, and helped other people to understand old writings in ancient languages. He first began thinking about photography in 1833, when on holiday on the lovely shores of Lake Como in Italy.

William liked to draw pictures of the scenery but he was a poor artist, so he used a box-like device called a *camera obscura*. This was the idea upon which Niepce had based his photographic cameras. Light coming from a scene went into the camera obscura and was reflected by a mirror, to project a picture on a piece of tracing paper placed over a sheet of glass. The picture was quite bright if it was looked at under a dark hood. William drew his pictures by tracing round the images projected on the paper. When he removed them, he was always disappointed. They were dull and lifeless, compared with the scenes on the paper. William felt sure that there must be a way to "catch" the scenes and keep them for all time.

Soon William heard that other scientists were making "sun pictures", by exposing light-sensitive paper to sunlight. These ideas were like those of Niepce and Daguerre, but at first William Fox Talbot did not know about their work.

He thought of a way to sensitise paper by dipping it in weak salt water, then drying it, before bathing the paper in silver nitrate. He placed objects such as leaves and pretty lacework on to the paper, and then exposed them to sunlight. After some hours of exposure, this method produced negatives in which the parts of the paper which received the light went black, and the unexposed parts stayed white. Now his problem was to stop the white parts from darkening after the objects were taken away. He needed something to fix the images. Quite by accident, he found that he could do this by dipping the paper into boiling salt water. Even with this fixer, the negatives eventually darkened all over, but later he used a chemical called sodium thiosulphate that worked very well. The "thiosulphate process", which is still used today, was invented by another Englishman.

The leaf and lace pictures were what nowadays we would call contact prints. When William tried using the sensitised paper inside a camera, his results were unsatisfactory. He realised he needed to concentrate the light. He did this by using a microscope lens that focused the light into a tiny box camera. His wife said it was just like a mousetrap! But inside that little "mousetrap", William obtained his first photographic negative taken of an actual scene. It was a picture of a many-paned lattice window in Lacock Abbey. Today that postage-stamp-sized negative is the oldest one left in the world—it is kept in the Science Museum in London.

As we know, Niepce and Daguerre had already managed to produce negatives, but *they* thought that negatives were useless. The Frenchmen were always trying to make realistic positive photographs directly. The "one-off" Daguerreotypes could only be copied by photographing them again, which was not very satisfactory. William Fox Talbot was the first man to invent a way in which a photographic negative taken with a camera could be fixed and then used to make any number of prints. He called his prints Calotypes.

William's idea was to put a properly-fixed negative on top of sensitised paper, and then to let light shine through on to it. The dark bits of the negative (formed from the light parts of the original scene) stopped light from getting through on to the light-sensitive paper. The light bits of the negative (formed from the dark parts of the scene) let light through. And there it was at last — a positive print which looked very much like the original scene. William Fox Talbot is famous for improving his methods of sensitising paper and for fixing images, but his greatest triumph was inventing the "negative-positive" way to print photographic pictures. It is still possible to print pictures from some of William's original negatives.

Even the French government was impressed by the Englishman's work, and in 1867 awarded him a gold medal. If you ever visit Lacock Abbey, you will be able to see William's lattice window — the original of the oldest photographic negative left in the world.

A picture of Lacock Abbey window, printed from William Fox Talbot's negative

Photography — without a Camera

You need:
blueprint paper (keep it covered with black plastic sheeting until you are ready to use it)
developer solution (store in a dark bottle, in a dark place)
a sheet of clear glass
a sponge
scissors
flat objects like feathers or leaves
a tray or piece of hardboard (to rest everything on)

Note — blueprint paper and developer may be bought from shops that sell reprographic materials such as are used by architects. Look for a local address in the Yellow Pages of the telephone directory under *Reprographic*.

What you do:
1 Put the paper — yellow side up — on the tray.
2 Arrange the feather or other object on the paper.
3 Cover both paper and feather with the sheet of glass.
4 Carry the tray carefully outdoors and expose the paper to sunlight until the yellow turns white (any time after five seconds).

5 Take the tray indoors again and sponge the blueprint paper with developer solution. (Always remember to wash your hands after using developer solution, and keep it away from your eyes.)
6 Finally, wash the paper in tapwater, and hang it out to dry.

Why People called Movies "the Flicks"

Did you know that half the time you are watching a movie, the screen is dark? Each second, twenty-five separate "frames" of still pictures are flashed on to the screen. But if the projector showed a continuously moving strip of film, you would see only a blur. So the film has to go through the projector in a series of jerks: the frames of the film are projected separately, one by one. And as each tiny picture is changing to the next, a shutter blocks the light, making the screen dark half the time.

You do not notice this happening because, after the eye has taken in a picture on the screen, the image can persist or stay in the mind for a fraction of a second. Scientists call this *the persistence of vision*. The mind holds the image until the next picture flashes on to the screen.

When a succession of pictures flash on to the screen, each one showing a separate part of an actor's movement, the brain "puts together" all the pictures, so that they seem to move.

In the early movies, too few frames went through the projector each second. The brain just noticed this, so the pictures on the screen seemed to flicker. Even today, you may sometimes hear a person calling movies "the flicks".

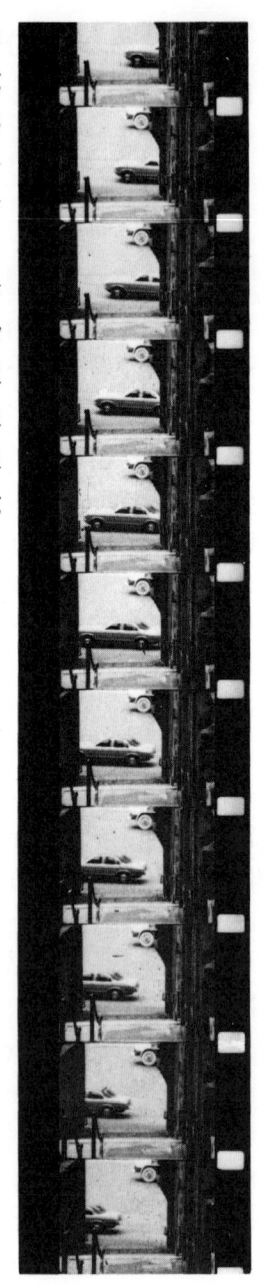

Captain Purefoy and the Large Blue

In certain secret places in the Cotswold Hills, and on north-west Scottish islands, there are little creatures that feed their own children to underground monsters in return for precious drops of a magical substance. The little animals are red ants, and the "monsters" are caterpillars — of Britain's rarest and most beautiful butterfly, the Large Blue. A hundred and fifty years ago, this butterfly was well known in several parts of the British Isles where the soil contains limestone or chalk. But by the beginning of the twentieth century the Large Blue was beginning to disappear, and until recently was thought to be extinct.

In fact, nowadays there are far fewer of all kinds of butterflies than there used to be. Changes in the weather affect their breeding, but the main reason why there are so few is that the weedkilling chemicals used by farmers and gardeners destroy the butterflies' food plants. Adult butterflies all feed on the sugary nectar from flowers, or on the juices of rotten fruit.

Another reason is the hobby of collecting butterflies. Butterfly collectors kill the insects and pin them on boards, to show off the beauty of their outspread wings. They use nets to catch flying butterflies, or search for their eggs on the various plants on which butterflies feed. Each butterfly prefers a particular food plant — the White Admiral likes honeysuckle, the Clouded

Yellow likes clover, the Chalkhill Blue likes horseshoe vetch, and so on. When a collector finds some eggs, he keeps them on the fresh leaves until they hatch. Then the caterpillars are fed on more of the special leaves, until they change into stiff chrysalises. Then comes the final *metamorphosis* (complete change) into adult butterflies. Perfect adults make the best specimens for collections. This hobby is not so popular as it was, because butterflies are scarcer than they used to be. Also, people are starting to realise that living butterflies are prettier and more interesting than dead ones. When it was realised that the Large Blue was *not* extinct in Britain, the public took a surprising amount of pleasure in the news.

But even in the days when the Large Blue was not rare, there was a little mystery about it. Collectors had difficulty in getting perfect specimens. They knew that the caterpillars fed on a plant with a pleasant smell and blue flowers, called wild thyme. There the caterpillars grew and split out of their old skins three times — but then they just seemed to vanish. Where did they go to? Nobody had ever seen a Large Blue chrysalis. Even collectors who raised the caterpillars from eggs never saw a chrysalis, for they found that after moulting three times, the caterpillars died.

The mystery was partly solved in 1915, when a Large Blue caterpillar bigger than any seen before was found inside the nest of some red ants. What was it doing there? How had it been fed?

The final answers to these questions were discovered

by a naturalist called Captain Purefoy. He patiently watched and waited to see just what happened to the caterpillars after their third moult on the thyme plants.

He found that a Large Blue caterpillar drops to the ground, where it wanders about until it is met and challenged by a red worker ant. He observed a strange kind of courtship, when the ant seemed to "milk" the caterpillar.

Later he learnt that the caterpillar could excite a red ant by stiffening two little "bumps" on its own rear end. This acted as a signal for the ant to begin tickling the caterpillar with its feelers. Tickling caused tiny drops of an oily substance to be exuded from glands inside the caterpillar's body. Drinking those drops sent the ant into a frenzy of pleasure.

Captain Purefoy was the first to observe how a red ant picked up a Large Blue caterpillar to take it down into the underground tunnels and chambers of the ants' nest. He noticed the way the caterpillar hunched its little body to make it easier for the ant to carry it in its jaws.

Hidden and protected from its enemies in the red ants' nest, the caterpillar is given newly hatched ant grubs to eat. To us, this is like a strange monster being given the ants' own children as food in exchange for the marvellous juice, but scientists remind us that animals should never be judged by human standards. The caterpillar must eat an enormous number of grubs, because in six weeks of feeding, growing and moulting, it trebles in size and becomes a pinky-white colour. After that it settles down in warm and drowsy contentment for a winter rest.

In the spring, the sleepy caterpillar is fed again. Eventually it becomes a yellow chrysalis, and three weeks later a Large Blue butterfly with folded wings emerges from the yellow skin.

Like a new aeroplane being wheeled from its hangar, the butterfly is escorted and helped by the ants to get above ground. There it climbs a stem, opens its wings to dry them, and flies away for a brief summer life. During summer the adult butterflies mate, and the females lay their eggs on thyme flowers, starting the cycle once more.

To find out about this astonishing life cycle, Captain Purefoy put Large Blue caterpillars inside the nests of a kind of red ant called *Myrmica rubra* (the "red ant that takes in guests"). Then he watched and waited, using all sorts of clever ways to see for himself what went on inside.

Nearly everything that is known about this rare butterfly was discovered through Captain Purefoy's patient observation.

Be a "Butterfly Watcher"

Stalk your butterfly by following it *quietly*. Don't shake any stems or branches where it lands, and keep your shadow well away from it. Watch it carefully. Does it keep its wings outspread when it lands, or does it put them together in an upright position? Does it keep slowly opening and closing its wings after it lands?

While your butterfly is feeding from a flower, try to get close enough to see how it sucks the flower's sweet juicy nectar. And does it always visit the same kind of flower, or does it visit different kinds?

What colour is it? What are its markings like? About how wide do you think the wings are when the insect is at rest? If you make pencil notes and sketches as you observe, they will help you to identify the butterfly from pictures in books.

Does your butterfly land on the same sort of place each time? Perhaps it settles often on the ground, or by a path, or on a fallen log — or it may settle on walls. Is it a fast or slow flier?

Butterflies prefer the open sunlight, and they seem to enjoy sunbathing. But where do they go in cloudy weather, or when it rains? Can you find out?

A very good place to look for butterflies is on the big droopy purple spikes of buddleia flowers, a common shrub in gardens. In a good "butterfly year", you might find a dozen or more, of several different kinds, on a single bush. Butterflies seem to get quite light-headed and become almost tame when drinking buddleia nectar. Sometimes, if you are very lucky, you may see a particularly fierce butterfly chasing the others away.

The Genius who Tamed Niagara Falls

In 1861, when he was only five years old, Nikola Tesla decided to become a genius. He wanted to be clever like his elder brother Dane, who had been killed in an accident. Young Nikki had overheard his parents saying how much they had looked forward to being proud of the wonderful things that Dane would surely have done, had he lived. There and then Nikola made up his mind. He was going to invent things which would amaze not only his home town of Smiljan, in Yugoslavia, but the whole world — and make his parents proud of him, too!

His first inventions came very soon afterwards. He made some toy pop-guns and sold them to the other children. This had to stop — because the people of Smiljan complained about the number of smashed windows! Next he tried to fly, but his homemade wings failed — Nikola fell and broke three ribs. Then he invented a motor which worked by the pulling power of six beetles glued to a small wheel. Although Mrs Tesla was pleased by her son's cleverness, she made him understand that using "beetle power" was cruel.

At seven years old, Nikola became a public hero. The family was living in the city of Gospic, which had just formed a new firefighting company. A day had been set aside for the new fire engine to be tried out, and everyone went along to watch.

Nikki walked all round the fire engine, very interested in the way it worked. It was a powerful water-pump, mounted on a cart, with two long handles (one on each side). Each handle needed eight strong men to push and pull it up and down, to bring the water up through the pipe which led from the river.

Nikola waited in the crowd as the mayor of Gospic gave a long and boring speech. Then a band burst into stirring music as teams of men started to pump the long handles. But no water shot from the hose-pipe's shining new nozzle, and Nikola began to laugh. Then he stopped suddenly, because he realised what was wrong.

Since the men were working so hard without result, the pump could not be sucking properly. The pipe must be blocked where it entered the river. Nikola ran down to the water and dived in, close to the pipe. There he could see that the end of the pipe had bent back, so that no water could get in. All Nikola had to do was to straighten the pipe, and he did so. Unfortunately, just at that moment the man holding the nozzle was pointing it at the mayor! Everyone laughed and cheered, and even the dripping wet mayor had to admit that Nikola Tesla was the hero of the day!

At school, when he was older, Nikola was so good

at mathematics that his teachers were convinced he was cheating. The truth was, however, that Nikola had an extraordinary talent which nobody has ever been able to explain. When he had a difficult sum to do, he could picture it in his mind. The numbers seemed to write themselves on a blackboard in his thoughts. He told everyone that the sum just did itself! When Nikola's father was sure that his son was telling the truth, he arranged for Nikki to be specially tested by his teachers, and they were amazed at his cleverness.

Nikola was still sure he wanted to be a genius — but he didn't know which *kind* of genius he wanted to be. Then, during long, lonely country walks, he became fascinated by all the energy running to waste in the mountain streams and waterfalls. He was also impressed by lightning, because he knew there was electricity in the blinding blue flashes. Nikola dreamed of controlling and using this energy.

One day his father gave him a book containing a picture of the mighty Niagara Falls between America and Canada. When Nikola saw that picture, he knew at last just what sort of genius he was going to be — an engineer. "One day I shall capture the energy from Niagara Falls!" he told his astonished father.

When he left school, Nikola went to a college at Graz in Austria, to study electrical engineering. There he was shown the famous Gramme machine.

The Gramme machine could be used as a dynamo to generate electricity. It could convert the energy from a steam engine or a waterwheel into electricity, which was a much more useful form of energy. The trouble was that the machine generated electric current that kept *alternating*, or changing direction, as the machine spun. To drive the electric motors of the day, this alternating current had to be changed into direct current — flowing one way all the time. This meant having to use a special part called a commutator, that produced electric sparks.

Nikola was clever enough to see that sparking wasted energy and made the machine less powerful. "Does it really need a commutator?" he asked his teacher, Professor Poeschl.

"Yes," said the professor. "All machines worked by electricity need direct current."

"But why not drive the machines by simply using alternating current, instead of wasting energy by converting it into direct current? Then you wouldn't need to have a commutator...."

Nikola's idea made the professor laugh so much that his glasses nearly fell off. Engineers had tried many times, and said it was impossible.

But on the day that Nikola left college, Professor Poeschl changed his mind. "Nikola, I believe your idea is right," he said. "I think that you will find a way to use alternating current for driving motors. Promise me that, when you do, you will tell me at once."

Some years later, on a winter evening in 1882, Nikola was walking with a friend. Suddenly he stood quite still and began to stare into the fiery sunset. "Watch!" he said. "Watch me reverse it."

His friend thought that Nikola had gone mad, and was trying to make the setting sun rise again . . . .

"Don't you see how smoothly it's running? Now I throw the switch, and it goes just as smoothly in the opposite direction." No, Nikola Tesla had not gone mad. Remember that strange ability of his to form pictures in his mind? After years of deep thinking and mental picture building, he had invented a motor which worked by alternating current. He could see it actually working in his thoughts.

Immediately he telephoned his old teacher at Graz. "Have you built a working model of the idea?" asked Professor Poeschl. He knew that no one else would believe Nikola unless he could demonstrate the idea with a model. Unfortunately that would cost money, and Nikola was poor.

Later on, by working for the Continental Edison Company in Paris, Nikola managed to earn enough money to do what he wanted. He employed people to make models of several different alternating current generators and motors that all worked much better than the direct current machines then in use.

Nikola's work on the old direct current machines for the Continental Edison Company saved the firm thousands of pounds, but they refused to pay all the money they owed him. Even worse, they weren't in the least interested in his alternating current machines.

Nikola felt that he was wasting his time. In 1884, he decided to try his luck in America, and he sailed for New York. He was twenty-eight years old, and he was almost broke — but he carried a letter of introduction to the American inventor, Thomas Edison.

When Edison met Nikola Tesla, he knew at once that this tall slim young man was a genius. One of Edison's great projects was already well under way — he was building power stations that would produce direct current to provide electric lighting in New York. He said that Nikola's alternating current machines would never replace direct current dynamos and motors — but he had an uncomfortable feeling that perhaps Nikola's ideas were far ahead of his own. Edison, the great inventor, who was making a fortune by improving other men's inventions, felt jealous of Nikola Tesla! However, since he did not want to lose a man with such a brilliant mind, Edison gave him a job.

Nikola was engaged to do some important work,

for which Edison promised to pay him a bonus of fifty thousand dollars. But when the work was finished, Edison pretended he'd been joking. He refused to pay up! So Nikola left the Edison Electric Company, but he could not find another job as an engineer. He had to earn his living by digging ditches — for two dollars a day (about 50p in those days). Then his luck changed at last. He was invited to speak before the American Institute of Electrical Engineers.

The speech given by Nikola Tesla in May 1888 was simple but impressive. Tesla's alternating current system, unlike Edison's direct current system, could generate thousands of volts. Millions, even! High voltages made it possible to transmit current many hundreds of kilometres from the power station — Edison's direct current system had a range of less than two kilometres! Nikola explained how motors and electric lights would work perfectly with his alternating current machines. He amazed his spellbound listeners by hinting that he could capture tremendous amounts of energy from Niagara Falls — and turn it into electricity! After a moment of stunned silence, the engineers stood up and clapped the world's greatest electrical engineer: Nikola Tesla.

Days later Nikola received a visit from George Westinghouse, who owned the Westinghouse Electric Company — a rival of the Edison Electric Company. Mr Westinghouse lost no time in offering one million dollars for the sole rights to build and sell forty of Nikola's alternating current inventions. Nikola accepted his offer, and used some of the money to build a laboratory. There he could work on those ideas which were still only vivid moving pictures in that remarkable mind of his.

George Westinghouse started building alternating current power stations that transmitted high voltage electricity across America. This meant that the direct current business was in trouble, and Edison reacted by trying to prove that alternating current would kill people.

All electricity can be dangerous if not used properly. To prove how safe alternating current and high voltages could be if sensibly used, Nikola said that he would pass a million volt current through his body! He demonstrated this many times at the Chicago World Fair of 1893, and people thought he must be a superman.

Then in 1895, a power station based on Nikola's ideas was built at Niagara Falls, at last keeping his old promise to his father. Nowadays all the world's big power stations generate alternating current. You use it whenever you switch on anything electrical.

Nikola worked in America for more than fifty years, until his death in 1943. During that time many of his mental pictures were turned into working machines. He had other ideas which he never managed to build, but he talked about them and wrote about them. Scientists are still working on these ideas, so that even though Nikola is dead, his work goes on.

Test Your Nerves with an Electric Circuit

What you will need
3 pieces of plastic-covered bell wire (2 measuring 20 cm, 1 measuring 60 cm)
An opened-out metal coat-hanger
A piece of wood measuring about $1 \times 10 \times 40$ cm
A 2.5 volt bulb in a bulb-holder
A 3 volt battery
Sellotape or plastic insulating tape
Screw-driver, scissors, screws, hand-drill

What you do
1   Bend the coat-hanger into awkward twists.
2   Force the ends of this twisty metal into holes drilled at each end of the wood.
3   Tape the battery to the wood. Also fix the bulb-holder to the wood, using small screws.
4   *Before making any electrical connections*, scrape the plastic off the ends of the wires.
5   Use one of the shorter pieces of wire to join one side of the battery to the nearest side of the bulb-holder. (Use your screw-driver.)
6   Also use a short wire to join one end of the twisty metal to the other part of the holder.
7   Scrape more plastic off one end of the longer wire. Use this long part of the wire to form a ring (about the size of a penny) around the twisty metal.

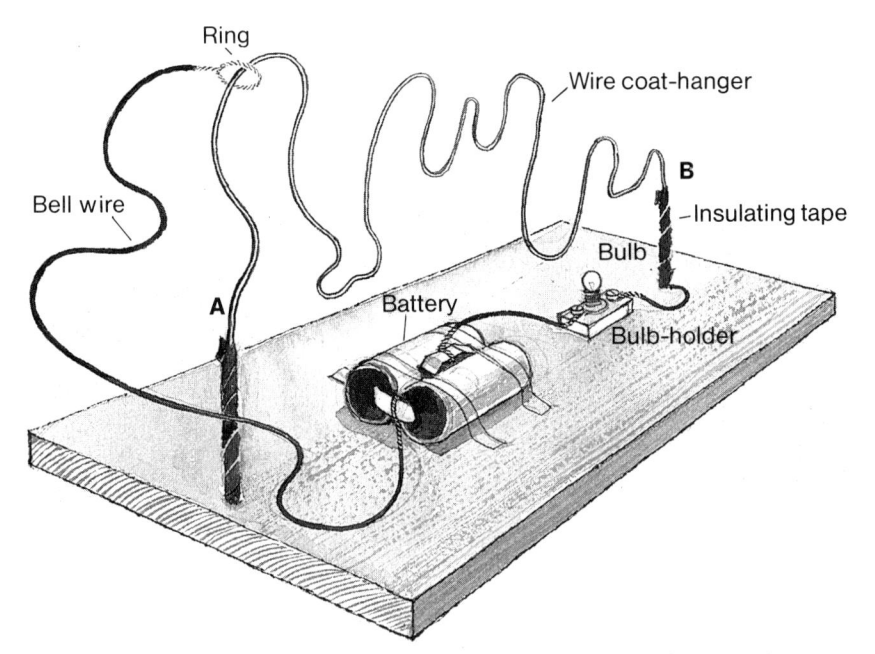

8 Then join the other end of the wire-with-the-ring to the battery.

9 Screw in the bulb. Now, whenever the bare ring touches the twisty metal, you make a complete electric circuit — and the light goes on.

10 Put some tape round the twisty metal at A and B, to make resting places for the ring (where it cannot make the light work). Unscrewing the bulb will also switch everything off.

The game is to move the ring from A to B, without making the light flash more than (for instance) three times.

You can make the game easier or harder by altering the twisty metal, or by changing the rules.

To do well at this game you need a very steady hand.

The Story of S

"Sorry if I'm late!" said the Memory Man. "The trouble is, I suffer from what many people would call 'the perfect memory'. And the last time I looked at a clock, the time was 4 p.m. In my mind, I can still see that clock's hands on 4 and 12, so in some strange way time has stopped for me, and I still keep thinking I'm early. It happens to me all the time. I never forget anything, ever! I'm sure I would be a much happier man if I were normal."

The man speaking was a Russian called Shereshevskii, who earned his living as a performing mnemonist (pronounced nem-on-ist), or "memory man". He gave his shows in theatres, travelling hundreds and thousands of kilometres between towns and cities in the largest country in the world. He was a sad and lonely man, but people who saw him performing thought that he was wonderful — a kind of magician.

We know about Shereshevskii through a Russian book called *The Mind of a Mnemonist*, written by a scientist — Professor Alexander Luria. In his book, Professor Luria called the man "S", and he wrote that working with S made him feel utterly confused.

With very little effort, S could remember long lists of numbers and silly nonsense words, called out by the people at his shows. If you asked him years afterwards, S could still repeat these lists. If you read him a long poem, even in a language he did not know such as Japanese or German, he could remember it perfectly.

S was quite unable to forget the most complicated mathematical formulas, after looking at them for only a very short time. He told Luria that the numbers and formulas appeared in his memory as if they were chalked on a blackboard. Nikola Tesla, whom you read about in the previous story, could also do this when he was a schoolboy. Like Tesla, all S had to do was to read the writing off the imaginary blackboard in his mind.

Professor Luria did not try to explain how or why S could do these wonderful things. He knew that of all the strange powers possessed by the human mind, memory is one of the strangest. Some scientists think that we are all capable of remembering everything that happens to us. They think that we do not actually remember everything because a part of the brain only lets us remember the things that are most important to us. All the huge number of unimportant details are quickly forgotten. This, they think, is so that we can make sense of a complicated world, and only think about the things which have meaning for us.

Other scientists do not agree. They think that it would be impossible for the brain to remember everything, because there are not enough brain cells to store all the different ideas. These scientists believe that information is stored in amongst the brain cells, in the same way that it is stored inside the magnetic memory of an electronic computer. They think that the size of our memory depends upon the number of brain cells we have.

If the first lot of scientists are right, S's mind could be explained by saying that his brain did not have the part that blocks out unimportant information. We do not know whether any of the scientists are right or not, because no one knows much about how the brain and human memory work. No one knows what part the brain cells and the nerves connecting them may play in our remembering.

About one child in ten has what is known as a "photographic memory". Perhaps Tesla was such a person. These children can remember whole pages from books they have read, because for them, remembering is like having the page in front of them once more — they have a "photograph" of the page in their minds. Usually they lose this ability when they grow up.

S's memory was not quite like that, because his memories were often mixed up with senses other than vision. Every sound he heard was changed by his mind into light and colour. If, during his memory act, there was a sudden noise in the theatre, the sound was changed into a picture in his mind of a white puff of steam. The mental picture was so vivid that the imaginary cloud of steam hid some of the numbers S was trying to remember. He once said of a certain man that he had a "crumbly yellow voice"!

When S was eating, his sense of taste kept getting muddled with his sense of vision. If he tried to read while he was having a meal, he found the words difficult to understand. This was because, as he told Professor Luria, "the taste of the food drowned out the meaning of the words". Reading itself was difficult, because every word he read caused his mind to fill with mental pictures.

If he started to read, "The boy is playing —", he immediately saw a boy surrounded by all sorts of toys. Then, when he read the rest of the sentence "— with his dog", S found he could not link the word "playing" with "dog" — because his mind was filled with images of many sorts of dogs.

S was unable to do any sort of ordinary job. He would have liked to be a musician, or a writer, but his fantastic mind made him a failure in both these professions. He had no choice but to be an entertainer.

But as a showman, S was amazing. His extraordinary ability to form mental pictures made all sorts of other kinds of magic possible. By imagining himself to be running very fast, for example, he could make his pulse beat faster. His pulse would actually quicken from seventy-two to over a hundred beats a minute!

Then by imagining himself lying in bed, he could bring his pulse down to sixty-five. By thinking that he was holding a block of ice, S could make one hand cold — while he made the other hand hot by thinking that it was resting on a hot stove.

S was always terrified of what might happen if the things he had remembered in the theatre yesterday came back to spoil his remembering in the show today. To try to stop this from happening, S wrote down all the memories from his show on a piece of paper, then he burnt the paper. In this way he hoped to destroy the memories of one day's complete show with the bright picture of the flames. Although this never worked, he was luckily always able to remember the right things in his performances.

The story of Shereshevskii is certainly a remarkable piece of evidence about the strange workings of the human mind. But he was never a happy man, and if you are a forgetful person, perhaps you will not feel so badly about it in future. Forgetting seems to have its own uses!

Walking Down Memory Lane

In his memory shows, Shereshevskii used to remember long lists of objects called out by people in his audience. One way he did this was to imagine that he was walking down Gorki Street in Moscow. As he heard each item, S made a mental picture, connecting the object with something he remembered about Gorki Street. If someone called out "A camel" for example, S might make a vivid picture in his mind of a camel sitting on the steps of the Gorki Street building he was just then passing on his imaginary walk. To recall the list afterwards, S remembered the "walk" and "saw" the objects where, in his imagination, he had placed them.

See how well *you* can do this memory trick. Get one of your friends to make a list of ten objects. Then have the items on the list called out, one at a time, while you imagine that you are walking to school (or along any street you know really well). Connect each object your friend calls out with something you are going past — a lamp post, a gate, or a tree — on your imaginary walk. Make your mental pictures as lively and funny as possible — this will help you to remember. Afterwards, just imagine that you are doing the walk again, and "seeing" the objects in their right order, as they appear in your memory.

Can you do the trick with twenty objects?

Isaac Newton

More than 300 years ago, on Christmas Day in the year 1642, a baby boy was born. His mother was a widow. Her name was Hannah Newton and her husband had died shortly before the baby was born. Hannah and her baby lived in a large stone farmhouse in a tiny village in Lincolnshire, near the town of Grantham.

Hannah called her boy Isaac. He was such a tiny baby that his mother said she could have put him in a large beer mug. He was often ill and Hannah had to make a stiff collar to hold his head up. But when this tiny baby grew up he became one of the greatest scientists there has ever been.

This story is not only about the important discoveries Isaac Newton made. It is also about some of the other things that made people interested in him. People who knew him couldn't understand some of the strange things he did. They knew he was a scientist but some of them thought he was a magician as well.

Isaac was a lonely little boy. He was an only child and when he was two years old his mother married again and moved to the next village. For some reason Isaac did not go with her; instead he stayed in the stone farmhouse with his grandmother. Perhaps because of this lonely life Isaac was a shy boy and he preferred reading and making his own mechanical toys to playing with other children.

There was no school in the village so Isaac did not go away to school until he was twelve. The Grammar School at Grantham was three hours away on foot and this was too far to travel every day, so Isaac stayed with a Mr Clarke. Mr Clarke kept a chemist's shop in Grantham and Isaac had a room at the top of the house where he kept his books and made his mechanical toys.

Although Isaac was a clever boy he was not much good at school. He was always bottom of the class, until one day something happened that made him work harder at his lessons. As he was walking to school Isaac Newton met the boy who was next above him in class. This boy was a bully and perhaps he thought Isaac was too small to stand up for himself. The bully attacked Isaac, giving him a terrible kick in the stomach. Isaac did nothing in return but all through the day he sat brooding about what had happened.

When school was over for the day Isaac challenged the bully to a fight. The bully accepted, sure that he would win. But he was wrong. Isaac was so angry and so determined that he managed to beat the bully hollow. Then, when he had won the fight, he determined to beat the bully at lessons as well. Soon he was getting high marks and doing better than the bully and all the other boys in the class.

Within a few weeks he was top of the school. But as soon as he reached the top he stopped working so hard and went back to his favourite hobby, making mechanical toys. He had started making these toys when he was very young but as he grew older his toys became both more complicated and more practical. There was a windmill set on top of Mr Clarke's house. There was a water clock for him as well; a clock that worked for many years and kept the time as accurately as the best ordinary clocks.

There were also toys made for fun. One of these was a kite that could carry a lighted candle up into the air. A box protected the flame and at night Isaac flew his kite high above the town of Grantham. When the people saw this strange flickering light in the night sky they were afraid — just as Isaac meant them to be. Some thought it was a comet. Others feared it was a ghost or even an evil spirit.

Isaac spent so much time making these toys that he lost his place at the top of the class. He went right back down to the bottom, but he did not stay there for very long. Once again he put aside his toys for a while and worked hard at his lessons. Soon he was top of the class again. All through his time at school he worked in this way, sometimes top of the class, sometimes at the bottom. It annoyed his teachers, but they did agree that a boy who could learn so easily must be very clever.

When he was about sixteen, Isaac left the school at Grantham and went to his mother's farm. She wanted him to help on the farm but farming was not something that Isaac was good at. He dawdled and daydreamed. He let the sheep and cattle stray. He was no good at business. Hannah was annoyed by his slowness, but she worried about him as well. Her son was no good as a farmer. He was too open and generous to be a businessman. He was not strong enough to be a soldier. He was only interested in ideas and inventions.

In the end she let him go back to school in Grantham. From there he went to Cambridge University. Hannah sent him what money she could afford, but Isaac had to earn most of his own money by working as a servant. He was still a quiet and lonely young man and his spare time was spent reading and working on his

Newton's telescope

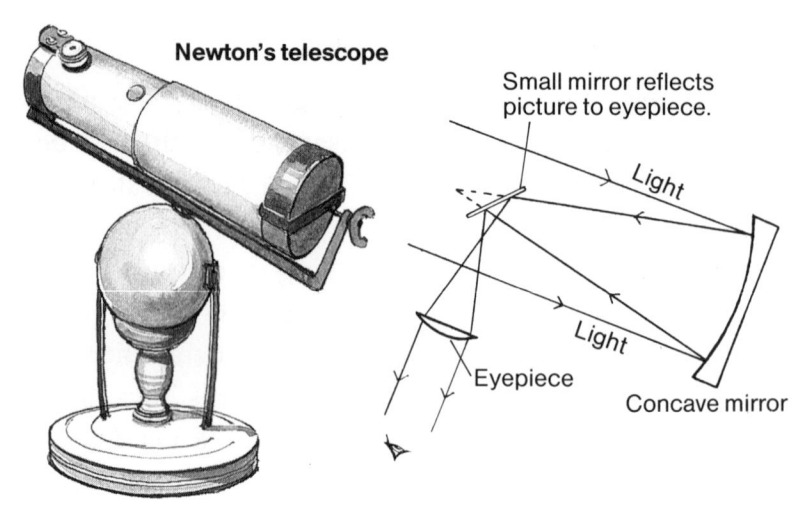

Small mirror reflects picture to eyepiece.

Light

Light

Eyepiece

Concave mirror

inventions. He still made things but now these were clever scientific instruments. He built his own telescope and used it for watching the stars and the planets. He began to study the way the planets moved in the skies. He thought about the paths they followed and tried to work out why they moved as they did. Already his ideas were far ahead of other scientists of his day but, being Newton, he told nobody about the telescope or his daring ideas.

Even though Newton kept his ideas to himself, one of his teachers did realise that this shy young man was something very special. Isaac Barrow, the Professor of Mathematics, encouraged and directed his brilliant pupil and slowly other people began to realise just how clever Newton was. His first years at the University came to an end in 1665 and if times had been normal he would probably have stayed on at the University. But times were not normal. In 1665 and 1666 a terrible sickness called the Plague swept across England. The University of Cambridge was closed and all the students were sent home. Isaac returned to Woolsthorpe, where his mother was still living, and spent the next two years there, thinking, studying and writing. During this time he worked out almost all his greatest ideas.

It was here in the orchard that the famous apple is supposed to have fallen on his head. Whether it did or not, he was led to think of the apple's fall as being like the fall of the moon through the sky and so to think of his theory of gravity. Newton's theory of gravity — that is, the pull of the Sun, the Earth and the planets on each other — is one of the greatest pieces of science ever worked out.

But Newton told no one about his ideas. Some things he kept secret for nearly twenty years.

In 1667 he went back to Cambridge and in 1669 he took the place of Isaac Barrow as Professor of Mathematics. As Professor, he had to teach other people and at last some of his ideas were spoken or written down for the first time. He chose to talk about light. Not many people came to listen and sometimes there was nobody at all, but Newton didn't mind. He was happiest in his laboratory, working on his experiments.

Rainbows fascinated him and he watched them in the skies and then in his laboratory. There he discovered what no one else had ever known; that white light is not white at all. It is a mixture of colours — red, orange, yellow, green, blue, indigo and violet. White light can be split into these rainbow colours by shining it through a glass prism. A raindrop in the air does the same thing and so produces the rainbows we see in the sky. He discovered too that it was possible to turn rainbow light back into white light. He shone light through one prism and then another. The first broke the white light up into the rainbow colours, the second turned the rainbow light back into white light.

Light was not his only interest. Each year he spent months studying alchemy, which is a very old form of chemistry. The aim of alchemy was to turn lead — a dark, heavy metal — into pure, shining gold, and alchemists had worked on this problem for hundreds and thousands of years. It was more like magic than science, but Newton spent his days and nights in the hunt for gold. In a glowing furnace he heated lumps of lead and mixed them with other metals and strange chemicals. In the glow of the furnace he must have looked like a magician and this is what some people thought he was.

At other times of year he turned back to his new telescope. Each clear night he watched the moon and the planets move through the sky. Nobody before had been able to say why the planets followed their particular paths. It was the riddle of the heavens, or so most people said. With the help of his telescope Newton solved this riddle, but he told no one about it. He kept the answer a secret because he thought that God had set the riddle specially for Newton to solve. Only years later did another scientist manage to get Newton to tell him the answer to the riddle of the heavens.

As Newton's ideas became known he became steadily more famous. All over Britain and Europe the name of Newton was known. His work in science brought him some friends but it also made him bitter enemies. Newton could become fierce when he was angry and he did not give up easily. His fight with the bully many years before had shown that. He had long quarrels with other scientists who argued against his ideas or who said that they, not Newton, had been the first to discover some new idea. All these quarrels made Newton even less willing to talk or write about his ideas. But at last, in 1685, a friend persuaded him to write down his answer to the riddle of the heavens. In three great books Newton explained the way the planets (and all other things) moved. He

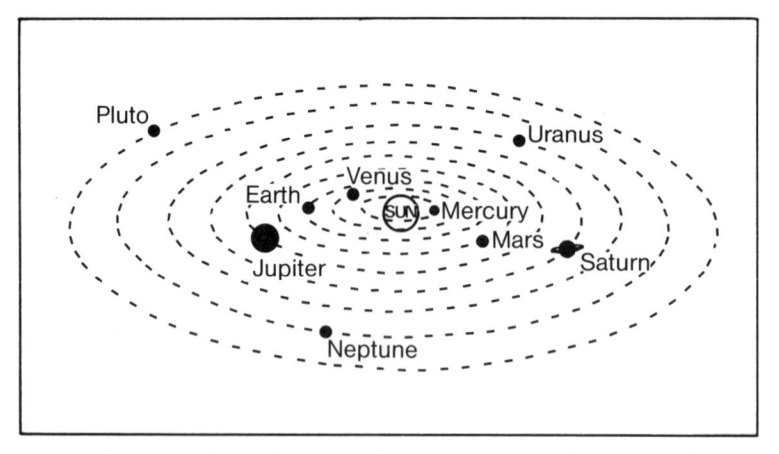

```
         Pluto                      Uranus
                    Venus
               Earth
                    SUN  Mercury
                           Mars
                  Jupiter         Saturn


                    Neptune
```

showed that the planets do not move in true circles but in ellipses. An ellipse is a flattened circle and the plan above shows this movement.

These three books made Newton the most famous scientist of his time. He became a Member of Parliament. He was given an important government job. He was even knighted, the first scientist to be honoured in this way. Instead of plain Mr Newton he became Sir Isaac Newton. Sir Isaac continued to write and experiment for the rest of his life. He was always able to solve in a few hours puzzles and problems that other people had spent months working at. His mind was active to the end of his life but it was no longer so clear and brilliant. All his great ideas came when he was still a very young man.

It is for these ideas that Newton is remembered today. He was certainly the greatest scientist of his time and probably the greatest British scientist of all time. That is why his picture is shown on the English pound note. You can still see him there with his telescope, his prism and one of his great books.

Rainbows on the Ceiling

When Newton shone sunlight through a glass prism, he found that the light split into the seven colours of the rainbow: red, orange, yellow, green, blue, indigo and violet. He also showed why a rainbow appears in the sky after a rainstorm when the sun shines. The little drops of water in the air all behave like little prisms.

You can make a rainbow on the ceiling, using only a shallow bowl of water, a small mirror and a torch. This is what you do.

Find a shallow bowl — a baking dish for example. Nearly fill the bowl with water. If you borrow a mirror, make sure you do not break it. Broken glass is dangerous and a broken mirror is supposed to bring bad luck. A sheet of shiny metal would do as well.

Rest the mirror, face side up, on the edge of the bowl so that it slopes into the water at an angle of about thirty degrees to the surface of the water. Get your torch ready.

Darken the room and shine the torch at the mirror. The light from the torch shines through the water and then is "bounced" or reflected by the mirror up to the ceiling. The water acts like Newton's prism and splits the light into its colours.

If the ceiling is very high you can hold a sheet of white card above the mirror.

On a bright, sunny day you may find that a glass full of water will also produce a rainbow on the wall. You can also see rainbow colours in oily puddles in the street and in soap bubbles. These rainbow colours are not made by prisms but by very thin films of oil or soap.

Halley's Comet

For thousands of years people were frightened by strange, fiery stars that seemed to come from nowhere and flash across the sky. Everyone knew that they were not ordinary stars for they had long, glittering tails that made them look like giant fireworks. In fact they were comets, travelling on paths that brought them near the earth only rarely.

Because they were so rare and so strange people often thought that they foretold great events. When a particularly bright comet appeared in the sky in 1456, special prayers were said in churches to save people from "the Devil and the comet". Another comet in 1531 was equally spectacular and just as frightening to the ordinary people.

When the first comet came in 1456 few people dared look too closely at it. In 1531 they were bolder.

Astronomers studied it closely. They noticed that its long tail always pointed away from the sun and they noticed too that the brightness of the comet varied. Some days it was very bright, on other days dimmer.

Yet another bright comet appeared in 1607. Still nobody knew what a comet really was and certainly no one knew that the comets of 1456, 1531 and 1607 were in fact one and the same. The first person to realise this was Edmund Halley, who had spent most of his life studying the stars.

• • • • • •

Halley was born in 1658, many years after the 1607 comet. As a child and a young man he was fascinated by the stars in the night sky, and by the time he was twenty he had his own seven-metre telescope. He took the telescope with him when he went to university and spent most of his spare time watching the sky. His stay at university was not a long one and after only two years he left to spend a year in a far-away island in the Atlantic Ocean.

The island of Saint Helena was a better place for watching the stars, and Halley preferred the stars to his work at university. Saint Helena was also a good place for watching comets, and by the time he was twenty-four Halley had studied many of these fiery stars. Some were very faint. They could only be seen through a telescope. Others blazed fiercely, so fiercely that they could even be seen in daytime.

In 1682 there was another particularly bright comet. Halley watched it through his telescope and decided that it was not a new comet. He felt sure it was the same one that had been seen in 1456, 1531 and 1607. Halley studied the comet and worked out its path. It went all the way round the sun and came back to the Earth about every seventy-six years. If you look at the dates 1456, 1531 and 1607 you can work out that these are either seventy-five or seventy-six years apart. Halley went on to say that the comet would appear again in the sky in 1758.

Halley died in 1742 so he was not alive to see whether he was right. But he was. On Christmas Day in 1758 the comet re-appeared and to honour his memory it was given his name.

Since then Halley's Comet has come back regularly every seventy-five or seventy-six years. It came back on time in 1835 and again in 1910 when it was seen for over a year. It is due back again very soon, in 1985. You will be able to check for yourself whether Halley was right.

The Story of RADAR

During the Second World War, the British fighter pilots won the Battle of Britain. This was the war in the air against the air force of Nazi Germany. The Germans had more aircraft, yet the British pilots managed to win. How did they do it? They even shot down German bombers at night. How could they "see" in the dark?

The answer is that they had radar. Radar is a radio "eye" that allowed the pilots to see enemy aircraft in the dark or long before they were visible to the eye. It was radar that played a major part in the Battle of Britain and helped save Britain from being invaded by the Nazis.

• • • • • •

This is the story of how radar was invented and of the man who invented it, Robert Watson-Watt, a Scots radio engineer. In 1934, Robert was forty-two years old, and a leading radio engineer doing work on finding out where "atmospherics", or radio crackle, come from. He was working for the British government, which was worried about the new leader of Germany, Adolf Hitler. Hitler had just come to power as the Nazi dictator of Germany and he seemed to be preparing for war. The Nazis said they had developed a "death ray" machine with deadly radio waves that could kill people and destroy cities. The British Government was not ready for war then and they feared

Hitler's air force and his "death ray" machines. So they asked Robert Watson-Watt to develop a British "death ray" machine to shoot down German bombers in the air — before they could reach British cities and bomb them.

Robert knew that there was no such thing as a "death ray" machine that used radio waves. He knew that you could not blow up aircraft with radio waves. But he had an idea. He thought he could build a machine that used radio waves to "see" aircraft in the sky at night. He quickly jotted down a few notes and made a few plans and drawings to show how such a machine might work. He called his invention *radar*, short for the initial letters in the words Radio Detection and Ranging. The word "ranging" meant "finding how far away the aircraft was".

Robert sent his radar idea to the Government and thought no more about it, for he was a modest man. To his surprise, the Government accepted his idea.

They asked him to develop his invention as soon as possible. They gave him money and a team of scientists and engineers to work with him.

The radar team began work in great secrecy near Daventry, not far from Birmingham. The Government were afraid that the local people might talk about what Robert and his team were doing and that the Nazis would get to know what was going on. So Robert told the local people that his team was trying to find a way to stop cars by radio.

The team worked hard to make Robert's idea work. They worked so hard and so fast that they made a radar set in less than six weeks. Radar must be one of the fastest inventions ever made!

It worked like this. They built a powerful radio transmitter which sent out a beam of radio waves in short "pulses" — rather like squirts of water from a water hose made by squeezing the hose pipe rapidly, or the flashes of light coming from a torch switched rapidly on and off. These radio pulses were very rapid, about a thousand pulses a second. The pulses shot through the air at the speed of light — until they hit a metal object such as a car or an aeroplane. This was the target. The pulses of radio waves were immediately bounced back, or reflected, by the target, just as a torch beam is reflected back by a shiny reflecting object. The pulses bounced back at the same high speed, hit the radar aerial and were turned into "blips" or dots on the radar screen, which was like a round television screen.

Robert worked out how to tell where the target was and in what direction it lay from the radar set. He could tell this from the position of the "blip" on the screen. The centre of the round screen showed where the radar set was. The farther out the blip was from the centre of the screen, the farther away the target was. By thinking of the radar screen as a clockface, he could tell the direction of the target by what hour of the clock it lay on. For example, a target in the direction of Birmingham might show up at twelve o'clock on the screen; so a target in the opposite direction would show up at six o'clock.

The team now had a radar set that showed the distance, or range, of a target and its direction. The next thing to do was to try the radar set out with a real target. They chose an aircraft. So they fitted up a van with a radar set and drove to a lonely spot in the country, well away from anybody who might spy on them and see what they were doing. They fixed up an aerial with a length of wire strung between two posts stuck in the ground. All was ready for the first radar test.

Robert had arranged for an aircraft to fly straight towards them from about a hundred kilometres away and at a steady speed. He knew how far away the aircraft would be at any time on its flight towards the radar van.

The aircraft took off and started flying in a bee-line for the van. At the same time Robert was staring at the radar screen. For what seemed an age he could see no blip on the screen. All the time the aircraft was flying steadily closer and closer towards the van. Then suddenly he called out happily: "There it is. A blip!" The direction was right.

Robert quickly worked out the range from the distance of the blip from the centre of the radar screen.

"Range: twenty-seven kilometres!" he said to his team. He checked the time on his watch.

They stood watching the blips getting closer and closer to the centre of the screen as the aircraft flew nearer and nearer to the van. Robert checked with the pilot how far his aircraft was at the time he saw the first blip on the radar screen. Sure enough, he was exactly twenty-seven kilometres away from the van. Robert was even able to work out how fast the aircraft was moving; for as the aircraft flew nearer and nearer, so the blips on the radar screen moved nearer and nearer to the centre of the screen. The faster the aircraft flew the faster the blips moved towards the screen's centre.

The next step was to build a more powerful transmitter and increase the height of the aerial so that it could pick up pulses from farther away.

The team very quickly built an improved radar set. With it they could track a flying aeroplane 120 kilometres away. The radar set was a complete success.

Robert reported the success of his radar machine to the Government. The Government immediately ordered several radar stations to be built along the south coast of Britain. In this way they could keep a round-the-clock lookout for enemy aircraft in the event of war.

Then a secret agent reported something upsetting from Germany. He had seen some very tall aerials being built. Were they radar aerials? Were the Germans on to radar as well? There was only one thing to do: find out. And who better to do so than Robert? So the Government sent Robert on a secret mission to look at the aerials. But how was Robert to carry out his mission without drawing suspicion on himself?

He decided to go with his wife, pretending to be bird-watchers on holiday. As bird-watchers they could carry binoculars and a powerful telescope without raising the Germans' suspicions. He and his wife dressed in country clothes and went on a long walking tour in the district where the aerials were being built. They soon found a church with a tall tower near the aerials. So Robert climbed to the top and using his powerful telescope took a closer look at the aerials.

"No, they aren't aerials!" he told his wife when he had climbed down from the tower.

In fact he was wrong. The Germans had begun to experiment with radar but they never caught up with the British — thanks to Robert's invention.

The British Government now ordered radar sets to be made on a large scale, in factories. As they had to keep it a secret, no one factory was allowed to build a complete set. Different factories had to make different parts of a set, without knowing what they were for. Then a team of radio engineers and scientists put the parts together to make complete radar sets. The team were sworn to secrecy.

In September, 1939, the war broke out. Thanks to Robert and radar, Britain was well defended by radar stations along the coast. These kept a round-the-clock watch on the skies and told instantly of the approach of enemy aircraft. Soon the British fighter and bomber aircraft had radar sets fitted in them so that the pilots could "see" the enemy aircraft long before they came into sight. In this way they were well prepared to attack the enemy. Then patrol vessels and other ships were fitted with radar sets so that ships patrolling the English Channel could spot enemy aircraft or enemy ships at long range.

In 1940 Nazi Germany was preparing to invade Britain. So they first sent their bombers to bomb British cities. British anti-aircraft guns, guided by radar, knocked out a number of the German bombers. But the job of defence rested with the British fighter pilots flying in their Spitfires and Hurricanes. In the summer the Battle of Britain began. France had fallen to the German army. Britain alone stood against the Nazis. It all depended upon the few British fighters to conquer the many German aircraft. The British fighter pilots were known as "the first of the few".

These few fighter pilots managed to shoot down the Nazi air force from the skies and so saved Britain from invasion. But they would never have succeeded without Robert's invention of radar.

Radar was a vital help for Britain and her allies all through the war, helping to win battles in the air, on the sea and on land. But radar is not just a weapon of war. Today it is used for helping aircraft take off and land in their thousands at hundreds of airports every day. Ships have radar to guide them through fogs and in stormy weather. Oil-rigs have radar to guide helicopters landing on their platforms in rough weather. Police can check the speed of motor cars with radar checks and traps. Radar is also used to make maps and for weather forecasting, and to guide spacecraft in their orbits through space. Radar is also part of most countries' defence systems against attack by nuclear missiles.

So from six weeks' brilliant work by Robert Watson-Watt has grown one of the most useful and accurate electronic machines known to man.

Hiroshima

The most deadly weapon the world had ever known — and they called it "Little Boy"! It was an atomic bomb, a Doomsday Machine created from some of the most wonderful ideas of science. It was the first of a range of weapons so powerful that they could destroy the world and bring death to people everywhere.

On the sixth of August, 1945, "Little Boy" was dropped on the Japanese city of Hiroshima, killing or injuring 240 000 people. It left those still alive with a terrible illness called radiation sickness.

Unlike earthquakes, floods or volcanic eruptions, this was a man-made horror, designed to end the Second World War.

Hiroshima was a Japanese military base in this war, which started in 1939 and was being fought by the Allies (Britain, Russia and America) against Germany and Japan. In 1945, when the war against Germany was over, the Japanese people refused to surrender. They said that they would fight the last great battle on the mainland of Japan, which could have meant millions of people being killed, on both sides.

By this time, the Allies had managed to invent and build an atomic bomb. They believed that by using it they could bring a quick end to the war.

On the morning of the sixth of August, 1945, when the seven rivers that ran through the harbour city of Hiroshima reflected the blue of a cloudless sky, observant people noticed a silver glint from an aeroplane high overhead. It was sunlight reflected off an American B29 bomber. Ironically, the aircraft which bore such a deadly load had a simple, cheerful name painted on its side — *Enola Gay*.

At 8.15 — the moment when the atomic bomb exploded 570 metres above the city centre — men and women were going to work, or shopping. Children were already in school. Soldiers and volunteers were busy preparing the city's defences.

The explosion produced a fireball 100 metres in diameter, with an unbelievable temperature of 300 000°C at its centre — 3 000 times hotter than boiling water! It was as if the sun had fallen. Wooden houses inside a circle of four kilometres across burst into flames, and the tremendous blast wave smashed down stone buildings. People who were in the open air beneath the explosion just disappeared, leaving only faint shadows on the broken walls and pavements.

Where people survived, they were so badly burned that their skins peeled and hung down. They looked like ghosts. Men, women and children were naked, for their clothes had been burnt away. Everywhere was filled with the sounds of crackling flames and the voices of hurt people calling for help. It was like Hell.

Soon after the explosion, Hiroshima grew dark as a huge mushroom-shaped cloud rose above the city. Then a warm rain began to fall, but the raindrops were stained black with dirt and dust. The black rain was poisonous, for it gave out deadly rays that made people ill. Purple coloured spots appeared on their skins, spreading to look like a map. This was radiation sickness, which killed many of the people who survived the explosion.

On the ninth of August, three days later, another atomic bomb was dropped on the military city of

Nagasaki. Soon afterwards the Japanese surrendered, and the Second World War was over.

Since then, more countries have learned to make atomic bombs and other kinds of nuclear weapons, all much more powerful than the original one. World leaders believe that great fears about the use of these horrifying weapons have prevented the start of another world war.

That first atomic bomb undoubtedly ended the war quickly in 1945. The people who died and suffered at Hiroshima and Nagasaki gave the world an unforgettable picture of what just one small nuclear weapon can do. We must never forget them.

But the invention of such weapons has posed an enormous problem for each person in every country which possesses one. How can we ever get rid of the atomic bomb? So long as our country has powerful enemies armed with nuclear weapons, can we afford to put ourselves in danger by giving up ours?

Scientific discoveries and inventions have made it possible for everyone in the world to live in peace and comfort. But science alone cannot solve the problem of a possible atomic war which no one could win. Unless the nations of the world all begin to work together for peace, it will never again be possible for anyone in the world to feel completely safe.

These are deep and difficult matters that none of us can ignore. But there is one way to begin — by making real efforts to care about the lives of all the other people on this crowded and troubled planet Earth.

Jane and the Apes

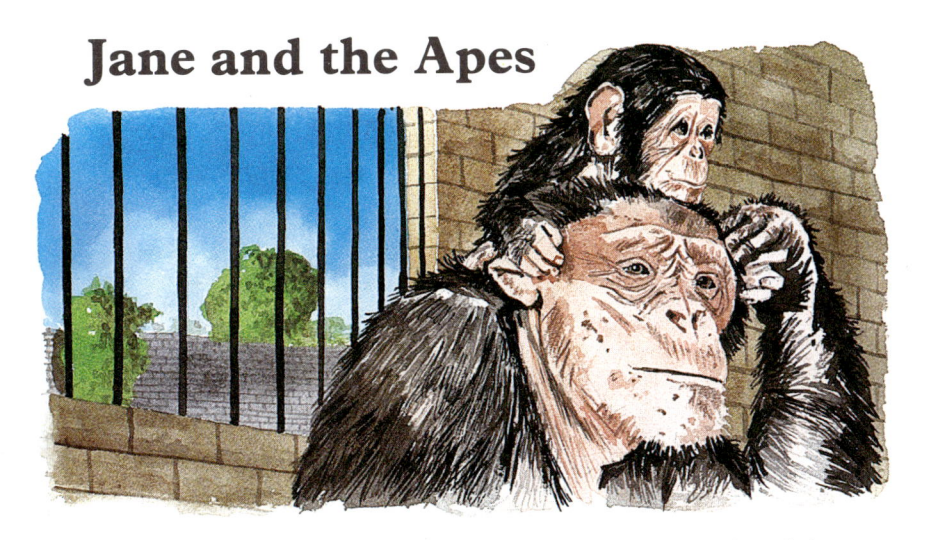

When the first baby chimpanzee ever to be bred in London Zoo was born in February 1935, a girl called Jane Goodall was not yet two years old. The chimp was named Jubilee, and its birth was a great event. It was widely reported in the newspapers, and toy chimpanzees became very popular.

Jane's mother gave her one of the large hairy toys as a present. This horrified Mrs Goodall's friends. They thought such an ugly thing would give the little girl bad dreams, but they were wrong. Jane called it Jubilee, and she loved it. She loved it so much that even now, although she is grown up and a famous scientist, she still treasures the battered and worn-out Jubilee.

The moment Jane could crawl, she became fascinated by animals. Once, when she was only four years old, she disappeared, and her mother grew so frantic with worry that she telephoned the police.

However, her little daughter was found safe and sound — inside a smelly henhouse, where she had gone to watch what happened when a hen laid an egg. Even at that early age, she had the scientist's habit of wanting to see for herself.

By the time Jane was eight, she had decided that when she grew up she was going to live with the animals in Africa. Her love for the hairy toy Jubilee, too, made her dream of getting to know more about wild chimpanzees, far away from the cages and compounds of London Zoo.

Some years after she left school at eighteen, Jane received a very exciting invitation. She was asked to stay with an old friend who lived in East Africa, in the country of Kenya.

During her holiday there, Jane met Dr Louis Leakey, a world-famous scientist. He was interested in the bones and other remains of prehistoric life — including the ancient ancestors of modern human beings. Although Jane had hardly any scientific training, Dr Leakey took her on as his secretary and assistant. He was sure that her love of animals and her deep interest in them would prove of great value to him.

While they were working together, Dr Leakey often talked to Jane about one particular community of chimpanzees. They lived on the shore of Lake Tanganyika, in what is now called the Gombe Stream National Park in Tanzania. Leakey knew that chimpanzees were intelligent, and he also knew that the bones of prehistoric human beings were often found on lake shores. He believed that a long and careful study of the Lake Tanganyika chimpanzees' family and community life might help towards understanding our own prehistoric ancestors.

Such a study would need tremendous patience. It would also mean hard work, in rough mountainous forest country, far from civilisation. Leakey confessed that he had been searching for twenty years for the right person to face the challenge. He wanted someone with a fresh mind, who simply wanted to know the truth. He did not want anybody whose mind was already filled with ideas and theories learned from books. He asked Jane if she would be prepared to do it. She was thrilled at the thought, and she agreed.

Dr Leakey then asked the Wilkie Foundation in Illinois, USA, to provide money to begin the work. This took all his persuasive powers, for Jane Goodall was both young and unqualified.

By the time she started to study them, however, Jane knew a great deal about chimpanzees. She knew, for example, that they may live for forty or fifty years in the wild state, and that they are more like humans than any other animal. Scientists believe that chimpanzees and humans had a common ancestor — which is not the same as believing that humans are directly descended from apes. But just like human beings, baby chimps have five years of infancy, when they need a mother's close care and protection. After that there is a period of childhood, followed by nine to fourteen years of adolescence, or "growing up". Chimpanzees reach old age at about thirty-five.

Affection between mothers and their children, and between brother and sister chimps, may last a lifetime. Father chimpanzees, however, take little interest in their young. The male chimpanzees are often bullying and bossy, and behave as though they are superior to females.

Jane started work at Gombe in 1960, and three months later she became ill with fever. Up to that point, she had found it difficult to get very close to the chimpanzees. The apes were afraid of her, and this depressed her. Nevertheless, as soon as she was fit once more, she was impatient to go on with her work.

Going out alone from her camp, she climbed a little mountain she called the Peak, to get a better view of her surroundings. She could see a group of chimpanzees feeding in some fig trees on the slopes opposite her, and she could hear screaming, barking and "pant-hooing" sounds coming from them. The noisy chimps swayed the branches as they swung effortlessly through the forest. Then she noticed another group, which included two baby chimps riding like jockeys on their mothers' backs. That day the chimps came very close to Jane, knowing perfectly well that she was there.

Her depression lifted, and in the weeks that followed, she began to recognise that the animals trusted her — but only in certain circumstances. If she watched them alone, if she always wore the same clothes, and if she never tried to interfere with them, the apes were prepared to accept her presence.

Another problem at first was that the local people at Gombe resented Jane. A rumour even spread that she was a spy sent by the government! As time passed, however, they learned to like and respect the brave and sincere "ape lady".

Jane loved her job. She was always amused by the antics of the chimpanzee youngsters. She enjoyed watching their wild games in the springy tree-tops, as they jumped and swung after each other with excited cries. Once she saw two tiny babies playing tug-of-war with a branch.

She noticed that as night-time approached, all the adults made individual nests for themselves in trees, by interweaving leafy twigs. New nests were made each night, and they were never fouled with dung.

The adults spent much of their time grooming each other's fur, picking out insects and bits of dirt. Although chimpanzees seemed to be very emotional, the friendly physical contact through grooming seemed to ease any tension between them. It made them relaxed, rested and peaceful.

Jane tried to work out why this should be. Perhaps, she thought, it was because of the years spent with their mothers. During those years, physical contact was reassuring and important, just as with human children. Then when the chimps began to grow up and to be independent, they found that grooming helped them to get on well with other chimps. Jane's chimpanzees used many surprisingly human gestures — gentle patting, hand clasping, hugging, and even kissing — to put one another at ease.

As Jane went on with her studies, Dr Leakey found some of her observations very exciting. She showed that chimps, like human beings, were omnivores, eating meat as well as vegetables and fruit. The Gombe chimpanzees fed on over ninety different kinds of leaves and fruit. They also ate termites, ants, caterpillars and bee grubs. They even raided bees' nests for honey. And they hunted in groups, working together to catch and kill larger prey such as bushbucks, baboons, monkeys and wild pigs.

One really important discovery was that the chimpanzees used tools. They used sticks in several different ways: to prise open bees' nests; to prod unusual objects like dead snakes; and to "fish" in the holes of termites' and ants' nests. Leaves were sometimes used to sop up water from waterholes, to pat wounds, and even occasionally as a kind of "toilet paper". This was direct evidence of tool-using by animals whose brains had not previously been thought capable of such intelligence.

Dr Leakey was very pleased that he had chosen Jane Goodall to do the chimpanzee study. Her fascinating discoveries proved very useful when he was trying to raise more money for the work, from sponsors such as the National Geographic Society.

In the course of time, Jane met and married a photographer named Hugo van Lawick. His brilliant pictures have helped to tell the world about Jane's research. Then Cambridge honoured Jane's work by giving her a doctorate (a PhD. degree). She became

Dr Goodall, and an "official scientist". By then she was world-famous. Her camp beside the foam-flecked, choppy waters of Lake Tanganyika was an important scientific centre. It attracted students from Europe and America, as well as from Tanzania.

Gombe was now Jane's home, but the years were uneasy with rebellions and wars. The African countries were fighting to gain their independence from European control. Across the lake, in the mountains of Zaire, Jane knew that there were bands of ruthless armed terrorists.

One night in 1975, about forty rebels crossed the lake in a little boat, and kidnapped four students as hostages. Although the students were eventually set free again, these were worrying days for Jane and her loyal assistants.

As if to emphasise the warlike nature of the world, Jane began to notice that her beloved chimps also made war on each other. Although her affection for them was as strong as ever, she no longer felt sentimental about them. She knew too much about them for that.

Jane and her team discovered that the chimpanzees in the area had separated into two rival communities. There were the southerners of Kahama, and the northerners of Kasakela. In time it became clear that the stronger chimps from the northern territory were gradually wiping out the weaker animals in the south. This "war of the apes" seemed to be over the control of hunting and feeding in the territory.

Male chimpanzees patrolled their boundaries in groups. Sometimes they would climb a tree to survey hostile ground, or would sniff at leaves and twigs as if searching for the scent of strangers. If rival groups met, they generally exchanged noisy threats, then moved apart without fighting. If a single chimp was encountered, however, or a mother with a baby, the lone animal was chased. It might even be attacked. Babies were sometimes killed in these attacks — Jane was horrified to discover that once in a while, a baby was seized and eaten by an adult chimpanzee. If a solitary childless female was set upon, she often reacted by joining the apes in the rival community.

All the chimpanzees under observation were given names. Goliath, for example, was an elderly southerner. One day he was attacked. He was pummelled and bitten for twenty minutes by five apes from the north. He was so badly hurt that he died.

One by one, other southerners were killed. While one called Madam Bee was dying, her daughter Honey watched over her. The younger ape kept brushing away flies from her mother's bleeding injuries. Then when Madam Bee died, Honey Bee put her ear to her mother's chest, as if she were listening for a heartbeat.

As has been said, Dr Leakey's hope was that Jane's study of the chimpanzees' behaviour might throw some light on why humans behave as they do. The observations of Jane Goodall and her staff over a period of twenty years on how chimpanzees bring up their children (and how abnormal chimpanzee youngsters behave) have already been of enormous value. They have helped psychologists, and doctors who specialise in mental illness.

Chimpanzees are very temperamental: violent one minute, and the next minute peacefully grooming each other. They appear to feel emotions very like ourselves — sadness, pleasure, curiosity and rage — but Dr Goodall has not yet been able to prove this.

Above all, the close study of chimpanzee behaviour may help us to understand just what causes the murderous and destructive violence that so often breaks out amongst human beings. It may help us to control that violence at last.

The Caged Scientist

Of all scientists, perhaps the one with the hardest life and the strangest life was a self-taught American, Robert Stroud. Robert was a strange and wild child and he had almost no schooling. When he was barely thirteen, he ran away from home and for the next six years he lived a wandering life; stealing rides on trains, sleeping rough, picking up odd jobs. He had no time for books; indeed he could barely write his own name or read a page of the newspaper. Then, one day when he was just turned twenty years of age, he picked up four lost baby sparrows. He cared for the sparrows, bathing and feeding them, and to his delight they lived. His was a lonely life and the birds gave him some company. Then he kept canaries. At first he had only two male birds, then he was given a third, a female called Jacky. The following spring Jacky had four babies and six years later Robert's bird room was home to 125 canaries.

Robert studied his birds with endless care, watching their short lives from birth to mating, from mating to breeding and then to death. He studied their feathers, their way of singing, their movements and their diet. Above all he studied their illnesses and before he was thirty he had found cures for three of the most serious diseases that affect cage birds.

All this would have been remarkable in any man, let alone one with no education or scientific training, but there was one other thing about Robert. He was a life prisoner in one of America's toughest jails, Leavenworth penitentiary. Eighty years ago prisons were grim places and Leavenworth was one of the grimmest. It was surrounded by a wall ten metres or more high and patrolled by brutal guards armed with heavy clubs. Here Robert was kept in solitary confinement. He was alone twenty-four hours a day and let out of his cell for just an hour a day to exercise. It was in the exercise yard that he found the four baby sparrows and it was in his tiny cell that he kept his birds and their cages. The cages he built himself, using only wood from old boxes, a broken razor blade, a small nail and a piece of broken glass. He had no microscope and no scientific equipment, but he still became America's greatest expert on cage birds.

• • • • • •

Robert's sad story really started in January 1909 when he killed another man in a fight. He gave himself up to the police at once and they shut him in the cells. From that date until his death in 1963 Stroud was never out of prison. Most of those years he spent alone in solitary confinement. He was never an easy man to deal with and early in his prison time he became sure in his own mind that he had been wrongly treated. He refused to accept the insults and harsh blows of the guards and in 1916 he killed one of them. Again it was a fight, again the fault was not all Stroud's. But the prison decided once and for all that he was a dangerous man. They ruled that he should be kept locked away from all human contact. For fifty years they never changed that fixed view, despite all the changes in Stroud's behaviour and way of life.

Few people can live in solitary confinement for very long. Their minds rot along with their bodies and only the proudest and strongest survive. Stroud was one of the strong ones. He was never much interested in other people and he put all his thought and care into looking after his birds. When there was one chance that he would be moved to another, more open prison he decided against it. "I can stand being alone," he said, "if allowed to study and improve myself." That is what he did. First he studied maths and painting. Then he found the baby sparrows in the exercise yard. A tree branch had fallen over the wall into the yard and with it came the broken nest. Robert caught beetles and flies to feed the tiny birds and added scraps from his own dull food when they seemed particularly hungry. He used a matchstick to set a broken leg on one bird. When the birds grew older and learnt to fly he trained them to come to him and to play tricks. At first the prison authorities knew nothing of his birds but one day Fletcher, the head of the prison, heard about what was happening in this tiny cell, and came to see this dangerous prisoner.

"Hello, Stroud," he said, peering through the spyhole in the door. "What is it?"

"Just a little something to show you," said Stroud. "Want to come in?" Fletcher nodded to the warder to open the heavy door, and came in slowly. The cell was badly lit and Fletcher saw nothing strange — only a narrow bed, a washbasin, and a barred window. Then Stroud snapped his fingers. At once two sparrows swooped down from nowhere on to his shoulder. He whistled and the birds dived for his shirt pocket. There they clung for a moment before flying away with beetles in their beaks. Then Stroud snapped his fingers again. This time the birds flew to the narrow bed. There was a white handkerchief spread there and they landed on it. For a moment they stood still, then they rolled over and played dead, their feet in the air. The astonished Fletcher laughed. What Stroud had done was against all the rules, but the prison head kept canaries himself and he was prepared to let the prisoner keep his pet sparrows.

That was Stroud's first victory over the harsh rules

of the prison. Canaries, perhaps because he knew that Mr Fletcher kept them, were the next. It took some months but in the end Robert Stroud had two canaries, Petey and Ape. From an old milk bottle he made a watering bowl. From a wooden soap box he made a cage — completely without tools. He cut the box into 128 separate strips, each over fifty centimetres long and laced them together to make his first cage. These first two birds were males and what Stroud then wanted was a female bird. Three weeks later he got one from a fellow prisoner who thought his bird was a sick male. When "Jack" was handed in through the cell door Stroud examined the bird closely and watched the way Petey and Ape began to behave. For no apparent reason they began to fight fiercely. "Jack" was really "Jacky", a female rather than a male.

A few months later Jacky laid her first eggs and Stroud's family of canaries began to grow quickly. At first all went well. Despite the poor food and the dark cell the birds grew fast. Every day Stroud took them out in cages to the exercise yard where they could feel the sunshine. Stroud studied the birds as they grew and read all the books in the prison library that had anything to do with birds. He even persuaded the library to take a magazine called the *Roller Canary Journal*. Greedily, he read the letters and articles every month. Then he began to write letters and enter competitions. At first he was only asking for advice and help, but soon he began to write to help and inform others. He began to make friends with other people who cared about birds, though none of them knew that Robert Stroud was a prisoner in Leavenworth. One of these friends sent him two special birds, which Stroud studied carefully. They looked healthy and they sang well but there was something about them that Stroud did not like. Nonetheless he let them mix with his other birds and for a few days all was well. Then he found that the two new birds were ill. From his books he worked out that the disease was incurable as well as very catching. What could he do? He could not move the well birds away from the sick ones — there was no room. He had no medicines to treat them with. He could not call on anyone else for help — they would not be allowed into the prison. Whatever he did it had to be done on his own. All he could do was to write letters to friends asking them to send supplies of medicines.

Each day more of his precious birds died and each day Stroud became more and more angry with his prison world. But he did not give in. He started instead to look for a cure to this mystery disease. He had eight different medicines and each one contained a different chemical. So, each day he tried a different chemical in a different amount. Still the birds died and Stroud cut open every one and made notes on what he found. Some chemicals lowered the high temperatures of the sick birds, others seemed to help the swellings on their bodies. As he experimented, Stroud began to work towards a cure: the right amount of chemical given at the right time and in the right way.

The cure did come in the end. It came when Jacky, one of his very first birds, fell ill. He packed her sores with one chemical, fed her the salt from another in the morning and yet another in the afternoon. He was determined that she should live, and amazingly, the old bird did. Two days later she was healthy again and showing no signs of the disease. The same treatment worked with other birds. He had found the cure to a disease that the experts said was incurable!

Not content with beating this disease he started to study others. Still working from his tiny cell he began to buy sick birds to treat and care for. By now Stroud was working eighteen hours a day to look after the 300 birds in his care. Perhaps for the first time, being a prisoner helped him. He was the only person in the world spending all day every day with his birds. There were no other jobs for him to do. There was no need to spend time cooking or cleaning. There were no other people to talk to and nothing to stop him watching his birds. Each morning he fed, watered and cleaned every bird. Then he checked their health and gave them their medicines. Afternoons were spent writing letters and articles or reading bird books. Then, in the evening, it was time to check all the birds again.

By 1929 all this work was bringing success to Stroud. His experiments, his observations and his careful notes helped him to cure two more dangerous bird diseases and to show what caused these diseases. Working alone, without a microscope, he had beaten all the experts. Even the prison authorities had relaxed. They still kept him alone in his cell but they allowed him to write his dozens of letters and articles and they let him have a few pieces of scientific equipment. They respected the way this man had changed from a dangerous killer to a peaceable scientist. Stroud was no longer violent but he was still a proud and stubborn man. As his fight with bird diseases had shown, he was not a man who gave in — ever. Soon this determination was to be tested.

In 1931 the Government sent a letter to the prison. It ordered Robert Stroud to give up his birds at once. It's hard now to know why they did this, since Stroud had become an example to all the Prison Service of how a dangerous man could be changed for the better. The prison authorities tried everything they knew to change the order but without success. Reluctantly they told Stroud the bad news. He must, said the Warden, "take immediate steps to get rid of his birds". Stroud was stunned. "Why?" he asked, "why?" The Warden could not say. He did not know. All he could do was repeat the order.

Stroud said nothing. Instead he began to think and plan. Silently he went back to his cell, silently he stared out of the window at the setting sun. Then, suddenly, he angrily turned to the old typewriter he had been given. For the next thirty hours he worked non-stop. He typed letters to bird clubs, to radio stations, to the Government, to newspapers. In each of his letters he stressed the discoveries he had made and the unfairness of the decision that the Government had taken. Then, with the aid of a loving friend, he smuggled the letters out of prison. Immediately Robert Stroud became news. From a forgotten man he became a national figure. Thousands of people signed an appeal to the President of the United States. Hundreds wrote letters of complaint to the newspapers and the Government. The newspapers wrote long articles about Stroud and his valuable work.

Eventually the Government was forced to change its mind and reach an agreement with Stroud. The birdman could keep his canaries. But that was not all. They gave him an extra room in which to keep them and they gave him the scientific instruments and equipment he needed for his work. He had won a great victory. It seemed that all was in Stroud's favour and he began to plan a new set of experiments and articles. But after a few weeks he began to have doubts about his "victory". He was allowed to write only two letters a week. There were problems about supplies for his birds. He had to smuggle his articles out of prison. Despite this he wrote — in sixty days — a full-length book about the diseases of canaries. That too was smuggled out of prison.

In this way Stroud continued his work. Thanks to the generosity of a bird lover outside the prison he was given a microscope, and with this he sought and found cures for yet more bird diseases. He built himself a machine for cutting microscopically thin slices from whatever object he wanted to study. All he had was a razor blade, some glass, a piece of hard wood and some pieces of metal. Like almost everything that Stroud tried, his plans worked.

Only in one thing did his plans fail. He could not persuade either the Government or the Prison service to free him from prison. As the years went by he became more and more bitter, more and more certain that he had powerful enemies who would never let him go free. His appeals were turned down. His pleas went unheard. Despite all the scientific work he had done and despite his good behaviour since 1920 he remained in prison. He had been there for thirty years when the Second World War started and he was to be there for twenty-four more. By 1939 he was nearly fifty years old. For ten years and more he had dreamt of being set free and running a bird business but it became clear that this was only a dream.

His birds were the only things he had to care about and he continued to read and write about them. Then, early one morning in 1942, even his birds were taken away from him. His cell door opened and an unknown guard came in. Stroud was told to dress, then he was handcuffed.

"O.K." said the guard, "let's get going."

"Go," said Stroud, "go where?"

"Places," said the guard.

Stroud was almost too stunned to speak but he pointed to his cages, his birds and his equipment.

"What about this?" he asked.

"What about it?" replied the guard. "Our instructions are that you walk out of here with nothing."

So Robert Stroud was marched out of his cell and away from his birds. The cell had been his only home for more than twenty years, the birds his only company for the same time. He was never allowed to keep birds again. A blow such as this might have killed another man. But not Robert Stroud. He lived on in prison for another twenty-one lonely years. When he died he had been in prison for fifty-four years and for thirty of those years his birds had been his only companions. Through his work he had made life better for cage birds everywhere. In saving their lives perhaps this caged scientist saved his own.

Index

activities   43, 51–52, 59–60, 70–71, 77, 87–88
airships   20–26
alchemy   84–85
ants   55, 57, 58–59
Arkwright, Richard   12, 14–19
atomic bomb   101–104

bald eagle   30–41
birds   30–41, 116–126
butterflies   55–56, 58–59, 60

Calotypes   49
camera   43, 45, 47, 49
camera obscura   47
canaries   116, 119–126
Captain Purefoy   57–59
carbolic acid   9–10
caterpillars   55, 57
chimpanzees   105–115
Clever Hans   27–28
colours of the rainbow   83–84, 88
comets   89–91

Daguerre, Louis   44–49
Daguerreotypes   46–47, 49

eagle   *see* bald eagle
electric current   64, 65–69
experiments   83, 84

factories   12, 16–19
film   43, 45, 53
Fox Talbot, William   47–50

germs   5, 8–10
Goodall, Jane   105–115
gravity, theory of   83

Halley, Edmund   89–91
Hiroshima   100–104

horse, talking   27–28

infection   6, 8–10

inventions   42, 45, 46, 49, 50, 61, 82, 94

Lake Tanganyika   107, 113
Large Blue butterfly   55–59
Leakey, Dr Louis   106–107, 111, 112, 115
Luria, Professor   73

memory   72–76, 77
Memory Man   72–76
movies   53–54

Newton, Isaac   78–86
Niagara Falls   63, 69
Niepce, Joseph   43–45, 49

operations   5, 6, 8

photograph   43, 44, 45, 50
photography   42–50, 51–52
Pfungst, Oskar   27–29
planets   82, 85–86
power stations   66, 67, 68, 69
prism   84, 87, 88

radar   92–100
rainbows   83–84, 87, 88

senses   74–75
sparrows   116, 117, 118–119
spinning   12–19
spinning machine   15–19
Stroud, Robert   116–126
surgeon   5–7

Tanzania   107, 113
telescope   82, 85, 90
Tesla, Nikola   61–69

water-frame   18, 19
Watson-Watt, Robert   92–100

Zeppelins   20–21